The Anti-Hustle Building A Thriving Business On Purpose & Wellbeing

The Anti-Hustle Building A Thriving Business On Purpose & Wellbeing

Robert Jakobsen

Published by Robert Jakobsen, 2025.

While every precaution has been taken in the preparation of this book, the publisher assumes no responsibility for errors or omissions, or for damages resulting from the use of the information contained herein.

THE ANTI-HUSTLE BUILDING A THRIVING BUSINESS ON PURPOSE & WELLBEING

First edition. January 2, 2025.

Copyright © 2025 Robert Jakobsen.

ISBN: 979-8230520245

Written by Robert Jakobsen.

The Myth of the Hustle

Breaking Down the Hustle Hype

You ever wonder why pulling an all-nighter is considered a badge of honor in the hustle culture? It's like a rite of passage, a demonstration of commitment and dedication. But let's break it down—does burning the midnight oil really lead to optimal results? Sure, there are those occasional crunch times where you need to go the extra mile, but glorifying constant sleep deprivation as a measure of success is seriously misguided. Let's be real here: the productivity gained from grinding away late into the night often pales in comparison to the increased inefficiencies and decreased creativity that result from exhaustion. The overrated all-nighter might give you a short-term boost, but it almost always leads to burnout and diminishing long-term performance. We need to shift the narrative and recognize that sustainable, consistent effort paired with ample rest and recovery is the true recipe for success. It's time to challenge the perception that success demands sacrificing every hour of sleep and leisure for work. Research consistently shows that our brains and bodies need downtime to recharge and perform at their best. So, next time someone starts boasting about their marathon work sessions, remember that there's nothing glamorous about neglecting your well-being in the name of hustle. As we navigate this modern era, let's redefine what it means to achieve. It's not about who can endure the most grueling schedule or clock the most hours; it's about who can deliver the highest quality work while maintaining a sense of balance and fulfillment. It's about striving for greatness without sacrificing your health and happiness along the way. Let's debunk the myth that the more we grind, the more successful we'll be. Life isn't a sprint—it's a marathon, and pacing ourselves with mindfulness and self-care will always win in the end.

The Overrated All-Nighter

Picture this: it's 2 a.m., and you're still hunched over your desk, fueled by copious amounts of coffee and sheer determination. You've been at it for hours, pushing yourself to the brink just to meet an impossible deadline. The allure of the all-nighter is strong—it screams dedication and commitment, but let's face it, it's overrated. Sure, there may be moments when burning the midnight oil seems like the only solution, but the truth is, the cost often outweighs the benefits. Seriously, when was the last time a brilliant idea struck you in the wee hours of the morning? The reality is that lack of sleep leads to sluggish thinking, reduced productivity, and a general feeling of being completely zombified. It's not a badge of honor; it's a cry for help. Imagine if, instead of scrambling to stay awake, you could approach tasks with a rested mind and fresh perspective. That's where the magic happens. So, the next time the temptation to pull an all-nighter creeps in, consider this: would a good night's sleep pave the way for a more innovative, energized, and effective you? The answer is a resounding yes. Besides, who doesn't love waking up without the heavy fog of sleep deprivation lingering over them? Trust me, your body and mind will thank you for it.

Money Doesn't Equal Meaning

Let's face it – we've all succumbed to the lure of the almighty dollar or the promise of a hefty paycheck at some point. It's easy to get caught up in the belief that financial success equates to a meaningful and fulfilling life. However, the truth is far more nuanced. While money can provide security and open doors, it doesn't automatically translate to a sense of purpose or satisfaction. Many individuals have chased financial gains, only to find themselves feeling hollow and unfulfilled. This isn't to say that money isn't important – it absolutely is – but it's essential to recognize its limitations when it comes to providing genuine fulfillment. Think about the times when you pursued a job or opportunity solely for the salary, only to realize that the work left you feeling empty and disconnected. It's a common experience that highlights the discrepancy between financial gain and personal fulfillment. By no means does this suggest that financial stability should be disregarded, but it does prompt us to reconsider what truly matters in the pursuit of a meaningful life. Perhaps it involves finding work that aligns with our values, fuels our passions, and allows us to contribute positively to the world. Maybe it requires defining success on our own terms rather than adhering to society's materialistic benchmarks. When we shift our focus from the relentless pursuit of wealth to creating a life rich in purpose and significance, the entire paradigm changes. We begin to explore avenues that bring us true joy, tap into our unique talents, and enable us to make a difference in the lives of others. As you navigate your journey, remember that while money can ease many worries, its role in crafting a fulfilling existence is only one part of the equation. It's the intangible qualities – like meaningful relationships, personal growth, and making a positive impact – that truly shape a life of depth and purpose.

Burnout Busters: Warning Signs to Watch

Alright, let's get real about burnout. It's not just feeling a bit tired or stressed; it goes beyond that. Burnout is like the big, flashing warning sign on the highway of life telling you to slow down and take a breather. So, what are some key warning signs to watch out for? First up, physical exhaustion. When you find yourself constantly fatigued or even getting sick more often, your body could be sending you a red flag. Then there's the emotional toll – if you're feeling disconnected, irritable, or overly cynical, it might be time to hit the brakes. Next, pay attention to your productivity taking a nosedive despite trying harder. Feeling ineffective or unaccomplished can signal burnout creeping in. Keep an eye on your attitude towards work because dreading going to the office or facing tasks could indicate burnout lurking around the corner. Finally, don't overlook changes in behavior or habits such as withdrawal from social interactions or reliance on unhealthy coping mechanisms. These are all vital indicators that it's time to make some changes before burnout takes control. Remember, recognizing these signs is the first step in preventing burnout from taking over. It's not a sign of weakness to address burnout; in fact, it's a courageous move in taking charge of your wellbeing and happiness.

Challenging the Grind Culture

Let's dig into the culture of grinding it out. There's this pervasive belief that success can only be achieved if you work yourself to the bone, neglecting self-care and personal time. This toxic mentality has seeped into our collective consciousness, making us believe that hustle is the only way to make it. But let's challenge that notion. What if we shifted the narrative? What if success wasn't about burning the midnight oil but about working smarter, not harder? It's time to debunk the myth that the grind culture is the only path to prosperity. When we glorify the grind, we overlook the detrimental effects on our physical and mental well-being. We sacrifice sleep, relationships, and even our health in pursuit of an unrealistic ideal. It's essential to recognize that there's more to life than endless toil. Instead of boasting about how many hours we've put in, let's celebrate efficiency, balance, and fulfillment. It's about finding the sweet spot between productivity and self-preservation. By challenging the grind culture, we empower ourselves to prioritize what truly matters—our health, relationships, and personal growth. Let's embrace a new approach—one that values quality over quantity and champions a sustainable, holistic definition of success. It's time to redefine the rules of the game and create a culture that honors well-rounded achievement, not just relentless hustle. So, let's break free from the shackles of the grind culture and pave the way for a more balanced and fulfilling journey toward success.

Quality Time or Countless Hours?

Many people have bought into the idea that grinding for countless hours is the only path to success. We live in a culture that glorifies long workdays and constant busyness, but it's time to challenge that narrative. It's important to recognize that working smarter, not harder, is the key to sustainable success. Quality time trumps countless hours of mindless work any day. When you prioritize quality time over countless hours at your desk, you can make room for creativity, inspiration, and rejuvenation. Taking breaks, spending time with loved ones, and pursuing hobbies are not distractions from success but rather essential components of a balanced life. Research has shown that taking regular breaks actually enhances productivity and mental wellbeing. It's about finding a healthy balance between work and personal life. Quality time allows you to bring a fresh perspective to your work, leading to better decision-making and innovative ideas. Some of the most successful individuals understand the value of downtime and leisure. They know that sustainable success is not achieved through burnout and exhaustion, but through intentional, focused effort. It's crucial to reassess your definition of productivity. It's not about filling every minute of the day with work but making each minute count. Embracing quality time empowers you to set boundaries and establish a realistic work schedule, contributing to a more fulfilling and sustainable career. When you shift your focus from logging countless hours to maximizing the quality of your time, you open yourself up to new opportunities and holistic growth. Quality always trumps quantity, not only in work but also in life. By prioritizing quality time, you're investing in your overall wellbeing and long-term success.

The Illusion of Busy

Have you ever found yourself swept up in the glorification of being busy? It's all too easy to fall into the trap of equating constant motion and packed schedules with success. But let's take a step back and really examine this 'busyness' that we often boast about. Are we truly being productive, or are we just spinning our wheels and perpetuating the myth that busier equals better? In reality, being busy doesn't always translate to being effective. We might find ourselves juggling countless tasks, attending multiple meetings a day, and staying in the office late into the night, yet still feeling unfulfilled or unsatisfied with our accomplishments. The sheer volume of activities on our to-do lists can give us a false sense of productivity while leaving us mentally and emotionally drained. This culture of busyness can also negatively impact our mental and physical well-being. Constantly rushing from one commitment to the next can lead to chronic stress, anxiety, and burnout. We may neglect our relationships, overlook our own self-care, and sacrifice our hobbies and passions in the name of keeping up with the relentless pace of modern life. Moreover, the 'badge of honor' mentality that often accompanies busyness can perpetuate a cycle of comparison and competition. We feel pressured to showcase our overflowing schedules as a sign of importance and relevance, inadvertently fueling a toxic cycle where everyone is vying to out-busy each other. It's time to challenge this illusion of busy and reclaim the narrative around productivity and success. Instead of glorifying busyness, let's shift the focus towards meaningful impact, efficacy, and balance. By embracing purposeful action and intentional prioritization, we can break free from the chains of busyness and strive for genuine fulfillment and accomplishment. So, the next time someone asks how you're doing, resist the urge to blur out "busy" as a default response. Let's start celebrating moments of rest, reflection, and genuine achievement, rather than perpetuating the myth that non-stop busyness is the ultimate marker of value.

What Really Drives Success?

Alright, let's dive into what really makes success tick. It's a common belief that working non-stop and being constantly busy is the key to success. But hold up – let's step back and reevaluate this notion. True success isn't about burning the midnight oil without end. It's not about juggling a million tasks without taking a breath. Real success involves finding balance, honing your craft, and focusing on what truly matters. When we talk about what drives success, it's not just about putting in long hours; it's about working smart, staying true to your purpose, and knowing when to take a breather. Success stems from meaningful connections, continuous learning, and the ability to adapt. It's also about embracing failure, because growth comes from those moments of falling short. So, as we explore what really drives success, keep in mind that it's not a sprint – it's a marathon. It's about making meaningful progress, maintaining positivity, and nurturing your well-being along the way. Remember, success isn't just about reaching the destination; it's about enjoying the journey and making a difference in the process.

Reclaiming Your Time

The myth of the hustle has led many of us to believe that success means sacrificing every waking moment on the altar of productivity. But what about reclaiming our time? In a world that glorifies busyness, it's easy to lose sight of what truly matters. Reclaiming your time isn't about laziness or procrastination; it's about prioritizing what brings you joy and fulfillment. It's about recognizing that time is a precious commodity that shouldn't be squandered on tasks that don't align with your values and goals. Picture this: instead of constantly chasing deadlines and living up to someone else's expectations, imagine having the freedom to spend your time on things that truly light you up. Whether it's pursuing a hobby, spending quality time with loved ones, or simply taking a breather, reclaiming your time empowers you to live a life that's meaningful to you. But how do you go about reclaiming your time in a world that seems designed to keep us in a perpetual state of busyness? It starts with setting boundaries and learning to say 'no' when necessary. It's about reevaluating your priorities and determining what truly deserves your time and attention. Sometimes, it means delegating tasks that don't require your unique skill set so that you can focus on what only you can do. It also involves recognizing the value of rest and rejuvenation, understanding that downtime isn't a luxury but a necessity for sustainable success. Additionally, embracing time management strategies can help you optimize your schedule and reduce time-wasting activities. This could mean adopting tools and techniques to streamline your workflow and minimize distractions.

Through intentional time management, you can create pockets of time for the activities that recharge and inspire you. Remember, the true essence of reclaiming your time lies in making room for the things that matter most to you. It's about rejecting the notion that success demands sacrificing your well-being and happiness. By reshaping your relationship with time, you can carve out a life that's defined by purpose, fulfillment, and a healthy work-life balance.

A New Narrative for Success

Let's shift the focus from glorifying burnout to celebrating balance and well-being. Success has been mythologized as a result of relentless hustle, but it's time to rewrite this narrative. Success is about achieving your goals and aspirations while living a fulfilling life. It's not about sacrificing your health, relationships, or sanity in pursuit of an abstract notion of success. A new narrative for success empowers you to embrace a holistic approach that values mental and physical well-being, meaningful connections, and personal growth alongside professional achievements. This doesn't mean slacking off or settling for mediocrity; it means redefining what it means to thrive in today's fast-paced world. In this new narrative, success is measured not just by financial gains, but also by the impact you make on the world and the legacy you leave behind. It's about finding harmony between work and personal life, prioritizing self-care, and staying true to your values. It's saying no to toxic hustle culture and embracing a mindset that champions productivity, creativity, and sustainable work practices. When we redefine success in this way, we unlock the potential for greater innovation, collaboration, and overall fulfillment. It's crucial to recognize that success is a journey, not a sprint. By fostering resilience, adaptability, and a growth mindset, we can navigate the inevitable challenges and setbacks with grace and determination. This new narrative encourages us to appreciate the process, celebrate small victories, and learn from failures. It acknowledges that our well-being and happiness are essential drivers of long-term success, both personally

and professionally. Moreover, this narrative extends beyond individual pursuits and encompasses the well-being of our communities and the planet. True success involves making positive contributions to society and practicing environmental stewardship. It's about creating businesses and systems that prioritize sustainability, equity, and social responsibility. When success is redefined in this inclusive and holistic manner, it becomes a force for positive change and collective prosperity. As we adopt this new narrative for success, we challenge outdated norms and pave the way for a more balanced, purpose-driven, and harmonious future. It's time to elevate well-being, connection, and authenticity as integral components of success, steering away from the glorification of burnout and relentless hustle. Together, we can build a world where success is defined by flourishing individuals, thriving communities, and a thriving planet.

Defining Your Purpose

What's Purpose Anyway?

You know, purpose is this big, buzzword these days, right? Everyone's talking about it, and it sounds like some magical cure-all for life's problems. But the truth is, a lot of people don't really understand what it means. See, purpose isn't just about having a lofty goal or a grand mission statement. It's deeper than that. It's about finding your unique reason for being, your own personal 'why' that drives you forward, gives your life meaning, and makes you jump out of bed in the morning. Without purpose, everything can feel a bit aimless, like wandering through a maze with no end in sight. But with purpose, suddenly everything clicks into place. Suddenly, you have direction, passion, and a sense of fulfillment. It's like turning on a light in a dark room. You see things differently, and it all starts to make sense. The thing is, though, figuring out your purpose isn't always easy. It's not something you can just Google or pick up off a shelf. It takes soul-searching, self-discovery, and a whole bunch of trial and error. And that's okay! It's all part of the journey. So, when we talk about purpose, let's remember it's not just a fancy word people throw around – it's the foundation of a meaningful, fulfilling life.

Why It Matters: The Big Picture

Picture this: you wake up on a sunny morning, feeling the energy of the day ahead. As you brew your coffee or tea, you take a moment to mull over what drives you, what makes you tick, and what gets you out of bed with a fire in your belly. That right there is your big picture. It's the canvas on which you paint your dreams, the roadmap that guides your choices, and the North Star that keeps you moving forward. Having a clear sense of purpose isn't just a feel-good sentiment; it's the fuel that powers your actions and decisions. When you understand why it matters, you're better equipped to weather the storms and revel in the sunshine along the way. Sure, it's easy to get caught up in the daily grind, but when you zoom out and see the grand tapestry of your life, that's where the real magic happens. Your purpose isn't just about you; it's about how you fit into the jigsaw puzzle of the world. It's about leaving your mark, igniting change, and making a dent in the universe. Without it, you're simply drifting through the currents, waiting for something to happen. With purpose, you're at the helm, steering your ship through uncharted waters with an unwavering belief in your destination. Sometimes, the big picture can seem daunting or fuzzy around the edges, but the beauty lies in the process of refining it, adding bold strokes, erasing the smudges, and marveling at the evolving masterpiece. When you know why it matters, the minutiae of everyday tasks gain significance. They become stepping stones toward something greater, rather than hurdles to grumble over. Purpose isn't reserved for the privileged few or the overnight success stories; it's a birthright, waiting for you to claim it. So, grab your brush, mix those vibrant colors, and start painting the big picture of your life – because when you step back and admire your creation, you'll see a story worth telling, a journey worth taking, and a purpose worth living.

Listen to Your Heart, Follow the Signals

Sometimes, amidst the chaos of everyday life, we forget to tune in to the whispers of our heart. It's easy to get caught up in external pressures or societal expectations that drown out our authentic desires. But if we take a moment to pause and listen, we might be surprised by what we hear. Our hearts have a way of nudging us towards what truly lights us up inside. Whether it's a subtle excitement about a particular project or a feeling of contentment when engaging in a certain activity, these are the signals we should pay attention to. The signs may be small at first, like a flicker of joy when discussing a particular topic or an unexplained drive to pursue a new hobby. These are the cues that our heart is sending us, guiding us towards the things that bring us genuine fulfillment. When we learn to recognize and honor these signals, we can start aligning our daily actions with our true passions.

This alignment can lead to a sense of purpose and satisfaction that transcends the mundane. It's not always easy to decode these internal signals, especially when the noise of the world is constantly clamoring for our attention. But by creating moments of stillness and introspection, we can start to discern the messages our heart is sending. Whether it's through journaling, meditation, or simply taking a walk in nature, finding ways to connect with our innermost thoughts and feelings can help illuminate our path. As we become more attuned to the whispers of our heart, we gain clarity on the directions we should take and the choices we should make. This isn't about abandoning responsibilities or pursuing fleeting whims; it's about integrating the wisdom of our heart into the practicalities of life. It's a journey of balance and harmony, where our innermost desires coexist with our external obligations. By listening to our heart and following the signals it offers, we embark on a quest towards living a more authentic, purpose-driven life.

Dream it Up: Visualizing Your Path

So, you've listened to your heart and soul, and now it's time to dream big. This is the fun part - let your imagination run wild and picture the life you truly want. Close your eyes and really envision it: Where are you? What are you doing? Who are you with? Paint a vivid mental picture of your ideal future. This isn't just wishful thinking; it's about setting a clear target for yourself. Visualize yourself achieving your goals, feeling the satisfaction, and relishing the success. Whether it's starting your own business, traveling the world, or making a real impact in your community, let your mind wander and dare to dream. Feel the excitement bubbling up as you think about the possibilities. But it doesn't stop there. Take those grand visions and start breaking them down into smaller, actionable steps. Dreaming without a plan is just daydreaming, after all. The key is to balance the excitement of envisioning your path with the practicality of mapping out how you'll get there. This step is crucial because it turns fantasy into reality. So grab a notebook or open a document, and jot down the details of your dreams. Describe it all - from the sights and sounds to the sensation of accomplishment. When you can clearly see it in your mind, the path becomes clearer too. Visualizing your path isn't just about dreaming; it's about laying the foundation for your journey. And once those dreams are solidified, you'll find yourself more motivated and focused on turning them into actual achievements. Get ready to take your aspirations and start making them real!

Aligning Passion with Practicality

So, now that you've dreamt it up and visualized your path, it's time to get into the nitty-gritty of merging your passion with practicality. This is where the rubber meets the road, where lofty dreams start to take shape in the real world. But let's be real – it's not always easy balancing what sets your soul on fire with what pays the bills. The key here is finding that sweet spot where your passion aligns with practicality. First things first – get clear on what exactly ignites your passion. What gets you excited every single day? Maybe it's a love for design, or a burning desire to make the world a more sustainable place. Whatever it is, identifying this passion is crucial. Once you've got that locked in, it's time to assess the practical side of things. What skills do you bring to the table, and how can they be applied to your passion? Are there opportunities in the market that align with your interests? It's all about marrying your enthusiasm with the realities of the world. And hey, if these don't line up perfectly at first, that's okay! Sometimes, it's about creating the bridge yourself. Maybe it means taking on a part-time gig to support your passion project, or seeking out mentorship to help shape your path. There's no one-size-fits-all approach, and that's the beauty of it. It's all about finding your own unique way to weave together what you love with what can sustain you. Embrace the journey, and don't be afraid to tweak your course along the way. Remember, passion and practicality aren't opposing forces –

they're dance partners in the intricate choreography of life. When you find that harmony between the two, magic happens.

Breaking it Down: Small Steps to Big Dreams

So, you've got this enormous dream, right? Maybe it's starting your own business, traveling the world, or becoming an expert in a particular field. It's exciting and daunting all at once because big dreams can be overwhelming. But here's the secret: breaking down those colossal ambitions into manageable steps can make all the difference. Think of it like climbing a mountain - you don't scale it all at once; you take one step at a time. First off, grab a pen and paper (or open up a digital note) and start jotting down every tiny task that could contribute to your big dream. Don't worry about order or feasibility at this point; just brainstorm and let your ideas flow. Now, pick out the small, practical actions from your brainstorm list. These are the building blocks that will get you closer to your ultimate goal. Once you've got your list, prioritize those mini-tasks. What needs to happen first? What can wait? By organizing your steps, you'll create a clear roadmap for progress. Remember, it's okay if things shift around as you go along. Flexibility is key. Time for the doozy: taking that first step. It might not feel significant, but it's crucial. It's like planting a seed for a mighty oak tree. Each small step builds momentum and compounds progress. As you tick items off your list, celebrate those victories! They're proof that you're moving forward, no matter how slowly. Of course, there will be roadblocks and setbacks. Expect them, embrace them even, as part of the journey. It's all about resilience and problem-solving. When something doesn't go to plan, pause, reassess, and adjust. There's no shame in altering your course if it serves your ultimate destination. In essence, achieving big dreams comes down to a series of small, consistent efforts. Your dream may seem far off, but with patience and persistence, those baby steps add up. So, lace up those shoes and start stepping – you're on your way to turning big dreams into remarkable realities!

Overcoming the Doubt Monsters

The journey to pursuing your purpose can often feel like a rollercoaster ride, complete with exhilarating highs and terrifying lows. One of the most common pitfalls along this path is encountering doubt monsters. These insidious creatures thrive on whispering negativity and fear into your ears, making you question your abilities and the validity of your dreams. But fear not, brave adventurer! You hold the power to overcome these doubt monsters and emerge victorious. First, recognize that everyone faces doubt at some point. It's a natural part of the human experience, especially when venturing into uncharted territories. The key lies in acknowledging your doubts without letting them take the wheel. Take a step back and examine the evidence supporting your doubts. Are they based on facts or mere speculation? Often, you'll find that doubts lose their strength when held up to scrutiny. Next, arm yourself with a shield of affirmations and positive self-talk. Remind yourself of past accomplishments and the unique strengths that brought you this far. Surround yourself with positivity – read inspiring stories, listen to motivational music, and seek out mentors who have conquered their own doubt monsters. Remember, you're not alone on this quest. Reach out to fellow travelers on similar journeys. Share your experiences and join hands in slaying the doubt monsters together. Witnessing others overcome their fears can bolster your own courage. Finally, embrace the discomfort. Growth and self-discovery seldom occur within the confines of comfort zones. Every triumph over doubt strengthens your resolve and fortifies your spirit for future challenges. The doubt monsters may persist, but armed with resilience and a supportive community, you possess the tools to diminish their power. Harness the energy of your doubts and transform it into unwavering determination. With each stride taken alongside uncertainty, you inch closer to fulfilling your purpose. So, stand tall, brandish your sword of belief, and face the doubt monsters head-on, for beyond them lies the treasure trove of your dreams.

Finding Your Tribe: The Role of Community

Let's talk about finding your tribe and the powerful role that community plays in shaping your journey. Think of your tribe as your support system, your cheerleaders, and your sounding board all rolled into one. These are the people who truly get you, who understand your ambitions and cheer for your victories. As the saying goes, 'Your vibe attracts your tribe,' so it's essential to surround yourself with individuals who lift you higher. This community can be composed of friends, family, mentors, or like-minded individuals who share your passions and values. The beauty of a supportive community is that it provides a space for collaboration and inspiration. It's where you can bounce ideas off each other, offer advice, or even find collaborators for your next big project. In times of doubt or uncertainty, your tribe can provide the encouragement and perspective needed to keep moving forward. Moreover, having a strong community reinforces the notion that you're not alone in your journey. When you celebrate successes with your tribe, the joy is amplified, and during challenging times, their presence acts as a source of strength. Remember, it's not just about what you gain from your community; it's also about what you give back. Being an active member of your tribe means offering support, lending an empathetic ear, and celebrating the successes of others. In doing so, you cultivate a reciprocal environment built on trust and encouragement. Finding your tribe takes effort, but it's a worthwhile investment for both personal and professional growth. Whether through local meetups, online forums, or networking events, take proactive steps to connect with individuals who share your passions and aspirations. Embrace the serendipity of these connections, and don't shy away from reaching out to potential tribe members. Always remember that your tribe doesn't have to be large; it's the depth of connection that truly matters. The bottom line? Cultivating a meaningful community enriches your journey, providing support, wisdom, and a network of kindred spirits to navigate the highs and lows of purposeful living.

Slaying the Procrastination Dragon

Procrastination, ah the nemesis of productivity! We've all been there, putting off tasks and delaying decisions because, well, Netflix seems more appealing, right? But fear not, for we hold the sword to slay this dragon. The first step is acknowledging that procrastination is perfectly normal. It's our brain's way of seeking pleasure and avoiding pain. However, when procrastination becomes a habit, it can hinder our progress. So, how do we vanquish this formidable foe? Start by breaking tasks into smaller, manageable chunks. This makes the horrid beast seem less intimidating. Set specific, achievable goals and reward yourself when you accomplish them. Create a conducive environment for work – a clutter-free space can do wonders. Limit distractions and use tools like timers to stay focused. It's also vital to address the root cause of procrastination. Are you anxious about the task? Fearful of failure? Understanding these emotions will help you tackle them head-on. Seek an accountability buddy or mentor who can provide support and encouragement. Sometimes, a simple pep talk goes a long way. Remember, perfectionism often feeds procrastination. Embrace imperfections and allow yourself to make mistakes – it's all part of the learning process. Finally, be kind to yourself. Accept that some days will be more productive than others, and that's okay. By leveraging these strategies, you'll chip away at the procrastination dragon until it's merely a harmless gecko. Now go, brave warrior, and reclaim your time from the clutches of procrastination!

Purpose is Fluid: Embrace the Change

Life is full of twists and turns, isn't it? Just when you think you've got it all figured out, something comes along and completely changes the game. Well, guess what? Your purpose in life is no different. It's not some static thing that's carved in stone; it's more like a living, breathing entity that grows and evolves as you do. So, if you're feeling a bit lost or uncertain about your direction, don't sweat it! It's all part of the glorious, messy, beautiful journey of finding your true calling. First off, let's debunk the myth that having a fluid purpose is a bad thing. In fact, it's quite the opposite! Embracing the change in your purpose opens up a world of possibilities and opportunities that you might never have considered otherwise. Think about it as a continuous process of self-discovery, where each new experience and insight nudges you in a slightly different direction. It's exciting, isn't it? You're not confined to one narrow path; you're free to explore and adapt as you go along. Now, let's talk about resistance. Change can be scary, especially if you've invested a lot of time and energy into a certain path. It's natural to feel a twinge of apprehension when faced with the unknown. But here's the thing: embracing the fluidity of your purpose doesn't mean discarding everything you've worked for. It's about integrating new elements into your existing framework, enriching your journey with fresh perspectives and insights. Remember, change isn't the enemy; it's the catalyst for growth and transformation. So, how do you navigate this ever-shifting landscape of purpose? Start by tuning into your intuition. Pay attention to those little nudges and whispers from within – they often hold the key to your next steps. Stay open-minded and curious, and be willing to entertain new ideas and possibilities. Surround yourself with people who inspire and challenge you, who celebrate your evolution instead of boxing you into a predefined role. Lastly, remember that it's okay to outgrow your previous versions. Just because a certain dream or goal no longer resonates with you doesn't mean you've failed; it means you've outgrown it, and that's a cause for celebration! Honor your past selves and experiences, but don't be afraid to shed old skins in favor of newfound clarity and purpose. Embracing the fluidity of your purpose isn't about starting over; it's about building upon the wisdom and resilience you've gained along the way. In essence, it's about welcoming change with open arms, knowing that each shift in your purpose brings forth new layers of growth and self-awareness. So, dear reader, take a deep breath, embrace the uncertainty, and trust that your ever-evolving purpose will lead you to remarkable places. After all, the most exquisite tapestries are woven from threads of change and adaptation.

The Wellbeing Advantage

Why Wellbeing Matters More Than You Think

You might have heard the saying, 'work hard, play hard.' But what about 'work hard, rest hard'? Wellbeing isn't just a nice-to-have; it's a must for true success. When you're constantly pushing yourself to the limit without taking time for your mental and physical wellness, you're setting yourself up for burnout and potential long-term health issues. Balancing work and life isn't just about finding time for hobbies or relaxation; it's about creating a lifestyle that supports your overall wellbeing. Studies have shown that individuals who prioritize their health and wellbeing not only perform better at work, but also experience greater satisfaction in all areas of their lives. So, it's time to rethink the old adage and start prioritizing your own wellbeing over the relentless pursuit of success. It's not selfish; in fact, it's essential for sustainable high performance.

Balancing Act: Work and Life Harmony

Achieving a harmonious balance between work and life is like trying to juggle multiple balls in the air without dropping any. It's not an easy feat, but it's essential for our wellbeing and happiness. When we talk about the balancing act of work and life harmony, it's about finding that sweet spot where your professional responsibilities and personal life coexist peacefully without one overshadowing the other. In today's fast-paced world, with the constant demands of work and the ever-present distractions of modern life, achieving this harmony can feel like chasing a mirage in the desert. However, it's not impossible. The first step is acknowledging that achieving work-life balance doesn't mean splitting your time equally between the two. It's more about setting realistic boundaries and priorities. One way to achieve this balance is by outlining your non-negotiables - things that are important to you outside of work. This could be spending quality time with family, engaging in hobbies you're passionate about, or simply having time for relaxation. By clearly defining these non-negotiables, you can structure your work commitments around them, rather than the other way around. Learning to say no when necessary is another vital part of maintaining work and life harmony. It's about recognizing your limits and being selective about where you allocate your time and energy. Sometimes, saying no to a work commitment means saying yes to your own wellbeing and personal life. Setting clear boundaries between work and personal time is also crucial. With the prevalence of technology, it's become increasingly challenging to disconnect from work. Establishing designated work hours and adhering to them helps create a separation between professional and personal life, allowing you to be fully present in each domain when needed. Finding balance also involves knowing when to unplug and recharge. Allocating time for self-care and relaxation is not a luxury; it's a necessity. Whether it's taking a walk in nature, meditating, or simply indulging in activities that bring you joy, making time for yourself is paramount to achieving work and life harmony. Remember, achieving work and life harmony isn't a destination; it's an ongoing journey. It requires continuous adjustments and evaluations as your circumstances change. Finding this balance will not only enhance your overall wellbeing but also lead to greater satisfaction and fulfillment in both your personal and professional life.

Mindfulness: Finding Your Calm in the Chaos

In today's fast-paced world, it's easy to feel like you're constantly playing catch-up. Mindfulness is the key to finding your calm amidst the chaos. It's about being fully present in the moment and cultivating a heightened awareness of your thoughts, feelings, and environment. When you practice mindfulness, you train your mind to focus on the here and now, rather than getting swept away by worries about the past or future. An easy way to start is by simply taking a few deep breaths and paying attention to the sensations in your body. Notice the rise and fall of your chest, the rhythm of your breath. This simple act can bring you back to the present and help you let go of stress and anxiety. Not only does mindfulness reduce stress, but it also helps improve your overall mental well-being. Research has shown that regular mindfulness practice can enhance self-awareness, increase emotional intelligence, and even boost creativity. Through mindfulness, you can develop greater clarity of thought and a deeper connection with yourself. It's a powerful tool for managing the pressures of entrepreneurship and nurturing a positive mindset. So, whether it's through meditation, yoga, or simply embracing moments of quiet reflection, integrating mindfulness into your daily routine can make a world of difference in how you navigate the ups and downs of the entrepreneurial journey.

Fuel for Success: Nutrition and Energy

Let's talk about food, glorious food! We all know that what we eat can have a big impact on how we feel and perform. Just like a car needs the right fuel to run smoothly, our bodies need the right nutrients to function at their best. So, what should you be eating to fuel your success? Well, it's all about balance and variety. You want to make sure that you're getting a good mix of fruits, vegetables, lean proteins, whole grains, and healthy fats. These foods provide essential vitamins, minerals, and antioxidants that keep your body running like a well-oiled machine. And don't forget about hydration! Drinking plenty of water throughout the day is crucial for maintaining energy levels and cognitive function. It's easy to reach for that extra cup of coffee when you're feeling tired, but staying hydrated is often the key to banishing fatigue. Speaking of coffee, while a little caffeine can give you a temporary boost, relying too heavily on it can lead to energy crashes and disrupt your sleep. Instead, try incorporating natural energizers like green tea or a handful of nuts into your midday routine. When it comes to meals and snacks, think of them as opportunities to nourish your body and mind. Plan ahead and prepare balanced, satisfying options that will keep you feeling fueled and focused. Remember, it's not just about what you eat, but also how you eat. Taking the time to sit down, savor your food, and enjoy the company of others can enhance your overall sense of wellbeing. Finally, pay attention to how different foods make you feel. Everyone's body is unique, so take note of how certain foods affect your energy levels, mood, and mental clarity. Learning to listen to your body's signals can help you fine-tune your diet for optimal performance. By prioritizing nutrition and making mindful food choices, you'll be setting yourself up for sustained energy, sharper focus, and enhanced resilience in the face of daily challenges.

Move Your Body, Lift Your Mood

Have you ever noticed that after a good workout or some physical activity, you feel more energetic and positive? That's not just a coincidence—exercise has an incredible impact on not only our physical health but also our mental wellbeing. When we move our bodies, whether it's through a quick walk, a challenging workout, or even some stretching, our brains release endorphins, the feel-good hormones that can lift our mood and reduce feelings of stress and anxiety. It's like a natural pick-me-up that can help us navigate the ups and downs of entrepreneurship. The best part? You don't need to be a fitness fanatic or spend hours in the gym to experience these benefits. Even a short burst of activity can make a difference. Maybe it's adding a morning stretch routine to your daily rituals or taking regular breaks for a brisk walk around the block. Finding ways to incorporate movement into your day can be a game-changer for your overall wellbeing. Plus, it's a fantastic way to break up long periods of sitting at a desk or staring at a screen, which we all know can take a toll on both body and mind. So, consider this your friendly reminder to schedule in some movement every day. Not only will it give you a boost of energy and motivation, but it can also spark creativity and help you approach challenges with a clearer, more focused mindset. Whether it's dancing to your favorite tunes, practicing yoga, or hitting the trails for a hike, find what feels good for you and make it a regular part of your routine. Your body and your mood will thank you!

Rest, Sleep, Repeat: The Secret Sauce

We've all experienced those days when we feel like we're running on empty. That's where the secret sauce comes in: rest and sleep. The importance of rest and sleep cannot be overstated when it comes to our overall wellbeing and success. When we prioritize rest, we give our bodies and minds the opportunity to recharge, repair, and rejuvenate. It's not just about avoiding burnout; it's about setting ourselves up for sustainable, long-term success. You may have heard the phrase 'I'll sleep when I'm dead,' but the truth is that insufficient sleep can significantly impact our health, cognitive function, and emotional wellbeing. So, let's debunk that myth right now and acknowledge that quality sleep is a powerful ally in our quest for excellence. Adequate rest and sleep are essential for our physical health. During sleep, our bodies perform vital functions such as repairing tissues, synthesizing hormones, and strengthening the immune system. Without enough rest, we become more susceptible to illness and find it harder to recover from physical exertion. In other words, rest is not a luxury; it's a necessity. Moreover, quality sleep plays a crucial role in our mental and emotional resilience. A well-rested mind is better equipped to handle stress, make sound decisions, and maintain focus. We've all experienced the mental fog that comes with sleep deprivation—missing keys, forgetting appointments, and struggling to concentrate. By prioritizing rest and sleep, we enhance our cognitive abilities and ensure that our minds are sharp and alert. So, what can we do to ensure we're getting the rest and sleep we need? First and foremost, establish a consistent sleep schedule. By going to bed and waking up at the same time each day, we regulate our internal body clock, which promotes better quality sleep. Additionally, create a calming bedtime routine that signals to your body that it's time to wind down. This could include activities such as reading, gentle stretching, or practicing relaxation techniques.

It's also important to create an optimal sleep environment. Keep your bedroom dark, cool, and quiet to minimize disruptions. Investing in a comfortable mattress and pillows can also make a significant difference in the quality of your sleep. Lastly, be mindful of your screen time before bed—putting away electronic devices at least an hour before sleeping can help signal to your brain that it's time to prepare for rest. In our fast-paced, hyper-connected world, it's easy to neglect the value of rest and sleep. However, by recognizing these as essential components of our overall wellbeing, we equip ourselves with the stamina and clarity needed to tackle challenges and seize opportunities. Remember, the secret sauce to success isn't just hard work—it's embracing the power of rest, sleep, and repeat.

Building Mental Resilience

Let's talk about mental resilience. It's like having a superpower that helps you bounce back from the challenges life throws at you. Building mental resilience isn't about avoiding difficult situations or suppressing your emotions; it's about developing the inner strength to navigate through tough times with grace and confidence. Here's the thing - setbacks, failures, and disappointments are inevitable, but how we respond to them can make all the difference. So, how do you cultivate mental resilience? It starts with acknowledging your emotions. It's okay to feel upset, nervous, or overwhelmed. Recognizing and accepting these feelings is the first step toward building resilience. Next, focus on reframing your mindset. Instead of dwelling on the negative aspects of a situation, try to find the lessons or opportunities for growth. This shift in perspective can empower you to move forward despite adversity. Another crucial aspect of nurturing mental resilience is self-care. Taking care of your mental health is just as important as taking care of your physical well-being. Engage in activities that bring you joy, whether it's spending time with loved ones, pursuing hobbies, or practicing mindfulness. Additionally, connecting with a supportive network of friends, family, or a mentor can provide invaluable emotional support during challenging times. Overcoming obstacles is also about being adaptable. Embrace change and uncertainty as opportunities for personal development. Finally, remember to celebrate your victories, no matter how small they may seem. Acknowledging your strengths and accomplishments fuels a sense of confidence and optimism, reinforcing your mental resilience. Think of mental resilience as a muscle that grows stronger with consistent exercise and nurturing. The more you practice strategies to build resilience, the better equipped you'll be to handle life's curveballs. Ultimately, developing mental resilience is an ongoing journey, and each experience offers a chance to reinforce this essential skill.

Digital Detox: Unplug to Recharge

In today's hyper-connected world, it's easy to fall into the trap of constant digital engagement. We're bombarded with notifications, emails, social media updates, and the allure of endless scrolling. It's no wonder that many of us feel overwhelmed and drained by the endless stream of information and demands for our attention. That's where the concept of a digital detox comes into play. A digital detox is all about consciously stepping away from the screens and technology that often dominate our lives. It's a chance to reclaim control over our time and attention, and to reconnect with the world beyond the virtual realm. This doesn't mean you have to go off the grid entirely – it's about finding a healthy balance and setting boundaries that allow for meaningful rest and rejuvenation. One of the simplest ways to start a digital detox is by scheduling regular 'unplugged' periods during your day. Whether it's an hour in the morning or the evening, designate a specific time when you'll disconnect from your devices and immerse yourself in activities that nourish your soul – be it reading, going for a walk, or spending quality time with loved ones. Creating this deliberate break from the digital noise can work wonders for your mental clarity and overall wellbeing. Additionally, consider setting boundaries around digital usage, such as restricting screen time before bed to improve the quality of your sleep. Try turning off non-essential notifications to reduce distractions and regain a sense of control over your attention. It's amazing how small changes in our digital habits can lead to significant improvements in our mental and emotional state. Another key aspect of a successful digital detox is finding alternative activities that bring joy and fulfillment. Take up a hobby that allows you to engage fully without the presence of screens, whether it's gardening, painting, or playing a musical instrument. Engaging in these analog pursuits not only provides a welcome break from technology but also fosters a sense of creativity and satisfaction that's often missing in the digital sphere. Lastly, don't underestimate the power of nature in facilitating a digital detox. Spending time outdoors, away from screens, can be incredibly restorative. Whether it's a leisurely hike in the woods, a day at the beach, or simply sitting in a park, immersing yourself in the natural world can help reset your perspective and recharge your energy. So, embrace the digital detox as a means to unplug from the chaotic online world and recharge in the simplicity and beauty of the offline reality.

Self-Care Isn't Selfish

As we navigate the hustle and bustle of everyday life, it's easy to neglect our own needs in favor of meeting the demands of work, family, and social obligations. But the truth is, prioritizing self-care isn't selfish; it's essential for our overall wellbeing. Taking time for yourself isn't a luxury—it's a necessity. When we invest in our own self-care, we're better equipped to handle challenges, manage stress, and show up as our best selves in all areas of life. Self-care comes in many forms, and it's highly individualized. For some, self-care might mean setting aside regular time for meditation or mindfulness practices. For others, it could be indulging in hobbies that bring joy and relaxation. It could even be as simple as making sure to get enough quality sleep each night. Whatever form it takes, the key is to prioritize activities that nurture your physical, emotional, and mental health. It's important to recognize that self-care isn't just about pampering yourself—it's about creating sustainable habits that support your overall wellness. This means setting boundaries, learning to say no when necessary, and cultivating positive habits that nourish your mind, body, and spirit. In a society that often glorifies busyness and sacrifice, it's crucial to reframe the narrative and remind ourselves that self-care isn't an indulgence; it's a vital component of a healthy, balanced life. By embracing self-care, you not only enhance your own wellbeing but also set a positive example for those around you. Demonstrating the importance of self-care to friends, family, and colleagues can inspire them to prioritize their own needs and lead healthier, more fulfilling lives. It's a ripple effect with far-reaching benefits. So, let go of any guilt or hesitation, and embrace the notion that self-care isn't selfish—it's a powerful act of self-preservation and self-love.

Creating Personal Wellbeing Rituals

We've all heard about the importance of self-care and creating personal wellbeing rituals, but why are these practices so crucial for our overall wellbeing? Well, think of personal wellbeing rituals as your secret formula for maintaining balance and happiness in your life. These rituals are the little acts of self-love and care that you integrate into your daily routine to nurture your physical, mental, and emotional health. They're like mini commitments to yourself, acknowledging that your wellbeing matters. Creating personal wellbeing rituals is a highly individualized process because what works for one person may not work for another. It's about finding what resonates with you and brings you peace and joy. Your rituals could be as simple as starting your day with a few minutes of gratitude journaling, practicing deep breathing exercises during moments of stress, or enjoying a calming cup of herbal tea before bed. The key is to make these rituals achievable and enjoyable, so they seamlessly become part of your daily life. When crafting your personal wellbeing rituals, consider the different aspects of your life that contribute to your overall happiness and fulfillment.

This could include physical activities like yoga, walking in nature, or dancing, as well as mental and emotional practices such as meditation, mindfulness, or engaging in hobbies that bring you joy. Remember, personal wellbeing rituals aren't just about temporary fixes; they're about building sustainable habits that support your long-term health and happiness. Once you've identified activities that resonate with you, create a schedule or routine that incorporates these rituals into your day. Consistency is key, so try to stick to your rituals as much as possible, even when life gets hectic. As you establish your personal wellbeing rituals, be open to experimentation and adaptation. What works for you today might evolve over time, and that's perfectly okay. The goal is to stay attuned to your needs and adjust your rituals as necessary. Additionally, don't forget the power of community and support systems. Connecting with like-minded individuals who value similar rituals can provide encouragement and accountability. Share experiences, exchange ideas, and learn from others to enrich your own rituals. Remember, creating personal wellbeing rituals isn't a one-time task – it's an ongoing journey of self-discovery and growth. Embrace the process, and let your rituals nourish and elevate every aspect of your life.

Strategic Efficiency: Working Smarter, Not Harder

Getting a Grip: Understanding What Matters

You know the feeling when you've been working all day but at the end of it, you wonder what you really achieved? It's like spinning your wheels in the mud, right? That's why understanding what truly matters is crucial. It's easy to get caught up in the small stuff that doesn't move the needle. But if you want to make real progress, you gotta identify those tasks that pack a punch and focus your energy there. So, take a step back and examine your to-do list. Ask yourself, 'What are the high-impact activities?' These could be things like closing a big deal, developing a new marketing strategy, or refining your product offering. Once you've identified them, make them your priority. Don't let the less important tasks steal the spotlight. By honing in on what truly matters, you'll find yourself making significant strides towards your goals, leaving the fluff behind in the dust. Remember, it's not about being busy; it's about being productive. And focusing on what matters most is the key to turning that busyness into true effectiveness.

Time Management Hacks: Because Time is Money

We all have the same 24 hours in a day, but how we use them makes all the difference. Time management isn't just about squeezing more tasks into your day; it's about making every moment count. So, grab your favorite mug of coffee and let's dig into some time management hacks that'll free you up for more of the good stuff. Ever heard of the two-minute rule? It's simple— if a task takes less than two minutes, do it now. This little trick can help clear your plate of small, nagging tasks before they snowball into larger issues. Another game-changer is the Pomodoro Technique—work for 25 minutes, then take a 5-minute break. Repeat this cycle four times and then take a longer break. It's incredible how this method can boost productivity and keep burnout at bay. And speaking of breaks, taking regular short breaks throughout the day can refresh your mind and prevent decision fatigue. Plus, it's essential to prioritize your tasks. The Eisenhower Matrix, named after the former U.S. President, helps you categorize tasks based on urgency and importance. By focusing on what's truly important, you'll make headway on your big goals. Let's not forget the magic of to-do lists. But here's the secret sauce—break down those mammoth tasks into smaller chunks and tackle one at a time. You'll be surprised at how rewarding it feels to tick off those mini milestones. Lastly, embrace technology. There's a wealth of apps and tools designed to streamline your day, from project management platforms to calendar apps. Give them a whirl and see which ones click for you. With these time management hacks in your toolkit, you'll be amazed at how much more time you have for the things and people that truly matter.

The Art of Delegation: Letting Go Without Losing Control

Delegating tasks can be a game-changer for any business owner or professional. It's all about knowing when and how to relinquish control without losing sight of the big picture. Delegation isn't just about offloading work; it's about strategic decision-making. So, let's dive into the nitty-gritty of this art form. First and foremost, identify your strengths and weaknesses. Delegate tasks that align with your team members' skills while freeing up your time for high-value responsibilities. Communication is key. Clearly define expectations, deadlines, and desired outcomes. Never micromanage. Trust your team, and provide support where needed, but avoid breathing down their necks. Empower your team to make decisions within the delegated tasks, fostering a sense of ownership. Regularly check in without imposing. Effective delegation hinges on understanding the capabilities and limitations of each team member. Address any obstacles hindering their progress and offer guidance where necessary, but resist the urge to take over. Set clear boundaries and encourage feedback. Lastly, celebrate successes and learn from failures together.

Delegation is not about shedding responsibility; it's about distributing it effectively for collective growth and success.

Tech Tools and Gadgets to Make Life Easier

Let's face it, technology has completely revolutionized the way we work and live. There are countless tech tools and gadgets out there that can genuinely make our lives easier and more efficient. From smart calendar apps that can schedule your appointments and reminders, to project management software that keeps everyone on the same page, there is no shortage of innovative solutions to help streamline tasks and save time. One game-changing gadget that has gained popularity in recent years is the smart speaker. With just a simple voice command, you can control your smart home devices, set timers, play music, get instant answers to your burning questions, and even receive daily briefings. It's like having a personal assistant at your beck and call! When it comes to productivity, nothing beats a good old dual-monitor setup. Being able to spread out your work across two screens not only enhances your workflow but also reduces the need to constantly switch between tabs and windows. It's a small investment that pays off big time in terms of efficiency. Speaking of efficiency, let's not forget about the wonders of cloud storage. No more worrying about losing files or carrying around heavy external drives – with cloud-based solutions, your documents, photos, and important files are accessible anytime, anywhere, as long as you have an internet connection. For those who are always on the go, having a reliable and feature-packed smartphone is non-negotiable. The latest smartphones come equipped with powerful cameras, sophisticated productivity apps, and seamless integration with other devices, making them indispensable for staying connected and productive. And finally, amidst all the high-tech gadgets and tools, don't overlook the simple yet indispensable ones like noise-canceling headphones, ergonomic keyboards, and wireless chargers. These small additions to your workspace can make a world of difference in terms of comfort and focus. In this digital age, embracing the right tech tools and gadgets can truly transform the way you work, allowing you to achieve more in less time while minimizing stress and maximizing efficiency.

Streamlining Processes: Cutting Out the Noise

We all know the feeling of being overwhelmed by a never-ending to-do list and drowning in a sea of tasks. It's time to take a step back, breathe, and start streamlining processes to cut out the unnecessary noise. Streamlining is about simplifying and optimizing the way we work, giving us more time and mental space for what truly matters. Let's dive into some practical strategies to achieve this. First off, it's essential to conduct a thorough audit of your current processes. Take a close look at every task and identify any steps that are redundant, time-consuming, or simply not adding value. This could be anything from excessive paperwork to repetitive manual tasks. Once you've identified these inefficiencies, it's time to roll up your sleeves and start eliminating them. One powerful way to streamline processes is by embracing digital tools and platforms that can automate mundane tasks. From project management software to customer relationship management systems, technology can be a game-changer in reducing manual effort and increasing productivity. The key is to carefully select tools that align with your specific needs and integrate seamlessly into your workflow. But streamlining processes isn't just about adopting new technology; it's also about reimagining how you approach your work. A fundamental part of this is breaking down silos and fostering collaboration within your team. By encouraging open communication and sharing knowledge, you can eliminate duplication of efforts and create a more efficient working environment. Furthermore, don't underestimate the power of standardizing procedures. Establishing clear and consistent processes for common tasks can significantly reduce confusion and errors, saving time and preventing costly mistakes. Whether it's creating templates for reports or defining standardized protocols, standardization can be a game-changer in streamlining your workflow. Lastly, continually seek feedback and monitor the effectiveness of your streamlined processes. Regularly check in with your team to identify any remaining pain points and areas for improvement. Remember, streamlining is an ongoing journey, not a one-time fix. By staying adaptable and open to evolving your approach, you can ensure that your processes stay lean and efficient in the long run.

The Power of Automation: Robots Aren't Just for Sci-Fi

Think about those everyday tasks that seem to eat up your time like a hungry monster. Now, imagine if you could have your very own robot to take care of them. Okay, so we might not be at the level of Rosie from The Jetsons (yet!), but automation is the next best thing. It's like having a virtual assistant who never needs a coffee break! One key aspect of automation is identifying repetitive tasks that can be done more efficiently. From responding to routine emails to managing your social media posts, there are numerous tools and software that can automate these processes. This frees up your precious time for the tasks that truly require your unique touch. Automation isn't just about saving time, it's also about reducing errors and ensuring consistency. When you set up automated processes, you minimize the risk of oversights or inconsistencies that often occur with manual tasks. Plus, it can give you a sense of control over your workflow, allowing you to focus on the bigger picture without getting bogged down in the nitty-gritty details. With the rapid advancements in technology, automation has become more accessible and user-friendly. You don't need a degree in computer science to implement automation in your business or personal life. There are countless resources, tutorials, and support available to help you harness the power of automation. So, don't let the fear of the unknown hold you back. Embrace automation, and watch as your productivity skyrockets and your stress levels plummet. It's time to bring your own robot army to the party—minus the metallic clanking and futuristic sound effects!

Batching Tasks: The Ultimate Time-Saver

Let's talk about the magic of batching tasks. No, it's got nothing to do with cooking up a storm in the kitchen (though that could be pretty magical too!). Batching is all about grouping similar tasks together and knocking them out in one go. Think about it – switching between different types of work or activities can be seriously draining on your brainpower. By batching tasks, you're saving yourself from wasting precious mental energy on constant context-switching. Whether it's responding to emails, making phone calls, or even doing chores around the house, batching can turn you into a productivity powerhouse. Imagine getting all your phone calls done in one go, rather than being interrupted throughout the day. Not only does it save time, but it also allows you to get into a groove – you'll find yourself becoming more efficient and focused as you tackle each similar task. Plus, the satisfaction of ticking off multiple items from your to-do list in one fell swoop? Priceless. For business owners, batching can be a game-changer. Set aside specific times for similar types of work, like content creation, client meetings, or administrative tasks. Simply put, it's all about finding your flow and staying in it for as long as possible. The benefits don't stop there – say hello to reduced stress levels and a newfound sense of control over your workload. Now, before you start thinking you need a fancy schedule or special tools to start batching, hold on. It's as simple as identifying your most common tasks, setting aside dedicated time slots for them, and sticking to your plan. Remember, the key to successful batching is staying disciplined and resisting the urge to deviate from your intended time blocks. So, whether it's work or chores, batching tasks can transform your efficiency and free up time for the things you love – like binge-watching your favorite shows guilt-free!

Learning to Prioritize Like a Pro

You know that feeling when your to-do list is longer than a CVS receipt? Yeah, we've all been there. Learning to prioritize like a pro is the game-changer you never knew you needed. It's not just about making a list and checking things off; it's about honing in on what truly matters and making sure those things get the attention they deserve. So, how do you become a prioritization master? First off, cut yourself some slack. No one expects you to be superhuman, so embrace the fact that some things can wait. Start by identifying the tasks or projects that align with your overall goals and values. If something doesn't contribute to your big picture, maybe it doesn't need to be at the top of your list. Next, consider urgency and importance. Is that looming deadline a bigger deal than researching new marketing strategies? Sometimes it's about putting out fires, and other times it's about investing in long-term growth. It's a balance. Another trick up your sleeve is the 1-3-5 rule. Choose 1 big task, 3 medium tasks, and 5 small tasks for the day. This method helps maintain focus while still allowing for flexibility. Don't forget to factor in energy levels. Are you a morning person who's on fire before 10 AM, or do you hit your peak after a cup of afternoon coffee? Schedule your high-energy blocks for the most important tasks. Lastly, embrace the power of saying no. It's okay to decline non-essential commitments when you need to preserve your bandwidth for what truly matters. Remember, becoming a prioritization pro is about finding your own flow and making space for what lights your soul on fire. It's not about fitting into someone else's mold; it's about creating a life and business that aligns with who you are and where you want to go.

Staying Flexible: The Key to Adaptability

In the fast-paced world of entrepreneurship, being adaptable is like having a superpower. It's all about embracing change and thriving in the face of uncertainty. Think of it as the ability to bend without breaking. Staying flexible means you can roll with the punches, pivot when necessary, and adjust your game plan on the fly. But it's not just about reacting to external factors; it's also about being open to new ideas and approaches. Flexibility breeds innovation and allows you to stay ahead of the curve. One key aspect of staying flexible is maintaining an open mind. This means being willing to consider different perspectives and be open to change. It's about recognizing that the landscape is constantly shifting and being willing to evolve with it. Another crucial element is being adaptable in your strategies and processes. This involves being prepared to iterate, experiment, and refine your methods continuously. It's about testing new approaches, learning from failures, and adapting your approach based on feedback and results. Cultivating adaptability also involves developing resilience. It's about bouncing back from setbacks, learning from challenges, and using adversity as fuel for growth. Being flexible allows you to weather storms and come out stronger on the other side. Embracing flexibility doesn't mean abandoning structure or discipline; it's about finding the right balance. It's the art of being organized while remaining agile, setting clear goals while staying open to detours, and sticking to principles while embracing change. Ultimately, staying flexible is about fostering a culture of adaptability within yourself and your team. It's about championing curiosity, creativity, and a willingness to embrace the unknown. The most successful entrepreneurs understand that adaptability is not just a survival skill; it's a competitive advantage. Those who can pivot and innovate will thrive in a rapidly changing business landscape.

Keeping the Fun in Efficiency: Work Smarter, Have More Play

So, you've streamlined your processes, mastered time management, and learned to stay flexible. Now it's time to inject some fun into your efficiency game! Maintaining a sense of enjoyment and playfulness amidst your quest for productivity is not just about having a good time—it's about sustaining motivation and preventing burnout. Let's dive into how you can keep the fun alive while working smarter. First off, it's essential to incorporate passion projects or hobbies into your work routine. Whether it's painting, gardening, or playing an instrument, allocating time for activities you love can infuse energy into your day-to-day tasks. Moreover, consider introducing gamification elements into your work environment. This could entail setting up friendly challenges with your team, using point systems to track achievements, or turning tasks into mini-games. By transforming mundane activities into exciting missions, you can boost morale and foster a sense of camaraderie among your colleagues. Embracing a light-hearted approach to communication is another vital aspect of infusing fun into efficiency. Encourage open and playful dialogue within your team, and don't be afraid to sprinkle some humor into your interactions. Laughter is known to decrease stress and increase creativity, so why not make your workplace a more joyful and vibrant space? Lastly, don't forget to schedule regular breaks for leisure and relaxation. Whether it's a quick game of ping pong, a stroll around the block, or a coffee break with a colleague, taking time to recharge throughout the day can enhance focus and overall well-being. Remember, maintaining a balance between work and play is key to long-term success and fulfillment. So go ahead, sprinkle some joy into your productivity game and watch as your efficiency levels soar!

Mastering Your Finances

Breaking Down the Basics: Know Your Numbers

Understanding the basics of personal finance is like laying a solid foundation for your financial future. It's all about knowing where your money comes from and where it goes. When you track every penny that comes in and flows out, you gain a crystal-clear picture of your financial status. This knowledge empowers you to make informed decisions about your spending, saving, and investing. Let's face it, no one wants to be caught off guard when it comes to money matters. By knowing your numbers, you can avoid uncertainty and take charge of your financial well-being. Whether it's managing bills, setting aside funds for future goals, or simply avoiding unnecessary expenses, having a grasp on your numbers puts you in the driver's seat of your financial journey. So, let's dive into the nitty-gritty of knowing your income, your expenses, and everything in between. It's time to break down those basics and take control of your financial destiny.

The Budget Blueprint: Making Money Work for You

Let's dive into the nitty-gritty of budgeting – a word that might make you groan but can also be your ticket to financial freedom. Here's the deal: a budget isn't about restricting your spending or giving up on life's little luxuries. It's about taking control of your money, so it doesn't end up controlling you. Think of your budget as a roadmap to get you where you want to go. It's all about making your money work for you, not the other way around. First, let's figure out where your money is going every month. The essentials like rent or mortgage, utilities, groceries, and transportation are non-negotiables. Once those are covered, look at your discretionary spending – the fun stuff like dining out, entertainment, and shopping. Challenge yourself to separate needs from wants. Now, armed with this intel, you can start crafting your budget blueprint. Allocate a portion of your income towards savings or paying off debts. And don't forget to build in some 'fun money' without going overboard. This is where you prioritize what's important to you, whether it's travel, hobbies, or building a rainy-day fund. Next up, monitoring your budget is like checking the gauges on a dashboard. Keep an eye on how you're tracking against your plan. If you overspend in one category, adjust elsewhere. Embrace the power of technology with budgeting apps or spreadsheets. Whatever method works best for you, stick with it. Remember, your budget isn't set in stone; it's a living, breathing document that evolves with you. As you gain more financial insights and your priorities shift, tweak your budget accordingly. The bottom line? Crafting a budget blueprint isn't just about crunching numbers; it's about creating a roadmap to your financial goals and dreams.

Ditching Debt: Raising the Financial Roof

Alright, let's tackle that looming cloud hanging over many of our heads—debt. It's like that stubborn grease stain on your favorite shirt—you just want it gone! But fear not; we've got the financial stain remover you need. First things first—take inventory of all your debts. Lay it all out there, from credit cards to student loans, and get a grip on the numbers. Once you've faced the music, it's time to formulate your battle plan. Prioritize your debts—whether it's the highest interest rate or the smallest balance, pick your target and make a plan of attack. Now, here comes the tough part—making sacrifices. Cut back on unnecessary expenses, tighten that budget belt, and throw any extra funds towards your debt. Trust us, that daily takeout coffee can wait. Another nifty trick is negotiating with your creditors for better terms or interest rates. Don't be afraid to pick up the phone and have that conversation. It could save you big bucks in the long run. And hey, if things are getting really tight, consider picking up extra gigs or a side hustle to funnel more cash toward your debts. Lastly, stay positive and track your progress. Celebrate every small victory—it's all part of the journey to financial freedom. With a sound strategy and some serious determination, you'll be sending those debts packing and raising the roof on your financial future.

Bank Smart: Saving Made Simple

Alright, let's dive into the world of saving and making your hard-earned cash work for you like a well-oiled machine. When it comes to banking smart, it's all about maximizing your saving potential without feeling like you're scrimping and saving every last penny. First off, set up different savings accounts for specific goals – whether it's for that dream vacation, a new car, or simply an emergency fund, having designated pots of money makes it easier to keep track and resist the temptation to dip into your savings for non-essential spending. Consider setting up automatic transfers from your checking account to your savings accounts each time you get paid, so that you're consistently building up those funds without even having to think about it. Next, take advantage of high-yield savings accounts or money market accounts that offer better interest rates than traditional savings accounts. While the rates may not make you rich overnight, every little bit helps in growing your safety net. Another key strategy is to shop around for banks that offer great perks like no-fee checking or low minimum balance requirements, as these can save you a tidy sum over time. Speaking of bank fees, keep an eye on those sneaky charges for things like ATM withdrawals, overdrafts, or paper statements, and opt for ATM networks that don't charge fees or find a bank that reimburses these costs. It's also essential to avoid unnecessary spending – especially on bank fees that can easily be avoided with a bit of vigilance. Lastly, consider meeting with a financial advisor to explore other savings options like CDs, IRAs, or investment opportunities that align with your financial goals. Remember, the goal here is to make your money work smarter, not harder, so get savvy with your banking choices and watch those pennies turn into pounds.

Invest Like a Pro: Letting Your Money Grow

Alright, let's dive into the exciting world of investing! When it comes to growing your money, you want to make strategic and informed decisions that will yield long-term rewards. Investing is like planting seeds in a garden – with care, attention, and the right conditions, those seeds can grow into flourishing plants. Similarly, when you invest wisely, you give your money the opportunity to grow and multiply over time. First things first, educate yourself. Before diving into any investment, take the time to understand the different options available – stocks, bonds, mutual funds, real estate, and more. Each comes with its own set of risks and potential returns, so knowing the lay of the land is essential. Next, consider your risk tolerance. How comfortable are you with the possibility of your investments fluctuating in value? This will help guide your decision-making process. If you're more risk-averse, you may opt for safer, steadier investment vehicles, while if you're willing to take on more risk for potentially higher returns, you might explore more aggressive options. Diversification is key. Instead of putting all your eggs in one basket, spread your investments across different asset classes and industries. This helps mitigate risk and allows for better overall portfolio performance. And hey, don't forget about the power of compounding. By reinvesting your investment earnings, you can accelerate your wealth growth through the magic of compound interest. Keep an eye on fees and expenses associated with your investments. High fees can eat into your returns, so opting for low-cost investment options can be a game-changer. Additionally, periodic review of your investment portfolio is crucial. As life changes, so too should your investment strategy. Rebalancing your portfolio ensures that it aligns with your current financial goals and risk tolerance. Lastly, stay patient and committed. Investing is a long-term game, and emotional reactions to short-term market fluctuations can lead to hasty decisions. Keep your eyes on the prize – building lasting wealth and securing your financial future. With careful planning and a solid understanding of investment principles, you can navigate the world of investing like a pro, letting your money work for you and pave the way for a prosperous tomorrow.

Tax Time Hacks: Keeping More of What You Earn

Hey there! Let's dive into some tax time hacks that'll help you hold onto more of your hard-earned money. First up, make sure you're taking advantage of all available deductions and credits. That means keeping organized records throughout the year so you can maximize those tax breaks come filing season. Next, consider contributing to tax-advantaged retirement accounts like a 401(k) or IRA. Not only does this help secure your financial future, but it can also lower your taxable income, putting more money back in your pocket. Another savvy move is to be mindful of any potential capital gains. If you have investments, consider timing their sale to optimize tax implications. Additionally, don't forget about the often-overlooked tax benefits for education expenses and charitable contributions. Oh, and stay on top of changes in tax laws—they can impact your tax strategy, so staying informed is key. Lastly, if tax lingo makes your head spin, it might be worth consulting with a tax professional. They can provide personalized advice and ensure you're making the most of every opportunity to minimize your tax bill. By mastering these tax time hacks, you'll be well on your way to keeping more of your earnings and feeling empowered when April rolls around.

Financial Forecasting: Planning for Rainy and Sunny Days

It's time to don your financial raincoat and sunglasses because in this section, we're diving into the art of financial forecasting. Picture this: you're on a hike, and the weather suddenly takes a turn. What do you do? You check the forecast beforehand and pack accordingly. The same principle applies to your finances. Financial forecasting is like your money's weather report – it helps you anticipate and prepare for the ups and downs. First off, let's talk about creating a realistic budget. This isn't about restricting yourself; it's about understanding your income and expenses. It's like mapping out the trail before embarking on your hike. Next, we'll look at scenario planning. Just as you'd pack an umbrella for potential rain, in finance, it's crucial to consider various scenarios – from unexpected expenses to opportunities for growth. We'll also dive into cash flow projections. Think of this as examining the terrain ahead – understanding when money comes in and goes out. As you forecast, consider both short-term and long-term goals. Short-term forecasts help you handle immediate challenges, while long-term forecasts guide your overall financial strategy. And remember, just like the weather, financial forecasts aren't set in stone. They're flexible and adaptable to changes. Ultimately, by mastering financial forecasting, you'll be better equipped to navigate through any financial storm and bask in the sunshine of financial stability.

Cash Flow 101: Keep the Currency Circulating

Alright, my friend, let's talk about cash flow. It's all about the dance of money in and out of your business. Picture this: your income as a river flowing into your bank account, and your expenses as streams that flow out. Now, the key is to keep that river flowing consistently and smoothly. You want to avoid sudden droughts or floods that could disrupt your financial ecosystem. So, how do you achieve this? First off, get a solid grip on your inflows and outflows. Track every penny coming in and going out. Use tools like accounting software or spreadsheets to visualize your cash movements. This insight will help you anticipate any potential surges or shortages. Next, consider your payment terms. Are you offering lenient credit terms to clients while dealing with strict payment deadlines yourself? Find the balance that keeps the current flowing steadily. Another vital aspect is managing your expenses. Look for areas where you can cut costs without sacrificing quality. Negotiate with suppliers, find efficient ways to operate, and keep a close eye on unnecessary spending. Maintaining a healthy cash flow involves staying on top of your invoices. Send them out promptly, and follow up on any overdue payments. Keep communication open with your clients to ensure timely settlements. And here's a pro tip: consider implementing incentives for early payments to keep the cash circulating. Now, what about the peaks and troughs in your business? Well, having a cash reserve acts like a buffer, providing stability during lean times. It's your financial safety net. Set aside a portion of your profits specifically for this purpose. Lastly, embrace the power of forecasting. Predicting your future cash flow will allow you to make informed decisions and steer clear of potential pitfalls. Keep adapting your strategies as your business evolves, and remember, maintaining a healthy cash flow is a journey, not a one-time feat. Treat it with vigilance, and you'll keep the currency circulating like a well-oiled machine.

Balancing Act: Juggling Earnings and Expenses

Alright, so here's the deal: managing your money is like performing a never-ending juggling act. You've got your earnings flying in from one side, and your expenses hurtling at you from the other. It's easy to feel like you're standing in the middle of a financial circus, desperately trying to keep all those balls in the air without letting any crash to the ground. But fear not – with the right approach and a dash of discipline, you can become the ringmaster of your own financial show. Let's break it down. First off, understanding your cash flow is key. Think of it as the rhythm of your finances – the pattern of money coming in and going out each month. By tracking this, you gain insight into where your hard-earned dollars are really going. Next up, it's time to craft a solid budget. This isn't about restricting yourself – it's about aligning your spending with your priorities and goals. Lay out your income and expenses, then give every dollar a job to do. You'll soon see that a well-crafted budget provides the balance beam you need to stay on track. Now, let's talk about that oh-so-important emergency fund. Life loves to throw curveballs, and having a safety net can mean the difference between a small hiccup and a major financial setback. Once you've got the basics in place, it's all about finding creative ways to increase your earnings while trimming unnecessary expenses. Whether it's picking up a side hustle or renegotiating your monthly bills, every little bit counts. And finally, remember to treat yourself once in a while! Finding that equilibrium between saving and splurging is crucial for maintaining your financial momentum without burning out. And there you have it – by mastering the art of balancing your earnings and expenses, you'll be well on your way to a more secure and stress-free financial future.

Financial Freedom: Living the Dream

So, you've navigated through the realm of balancing your earnings and expenses. Now, let's set our sights on the ultimate destination - financial freedom. Picture this: you wake up in the morning, not to an alarm clock, but to the soothing luxury of knowing that every aspect of your life is taken care of. You have the means to pursue your passions, indulge in hobbies, travel at will, and support causes that resonate with you. Achieving financial freedom isn't about hoarding wealth or living extravagantly; it's about having the autonomy and security to live life on your own terms. To embark on this journey, it's crucial to fully comprehend what financial freedom means to you personally. For some, it may entail being debt-free, while for others, it could mean having a robust investment portfolio. Understanding your definition of financial freedom will steer your objectives and decisions towards aligning with this vision. One of the fundamental pillars of attaining financial freedom is smart investment. This involves leveraging your resources to generate passive income streams. Whether it's through real estate, stocks, bonds, or entrepreneurship, the goal is to make money work for you, even while you're off chasing other aspirations. Think of it as planting seeds today to reap a bountiful harvest tomorrow. Moreover, simplifying your life plays a pivotal role in the pursuit of financial freedom. Adopting a minimalist mindset can liberate you from the burden of material possessions and unnecessary expenses. By curating a lifestyle that prioritizes experiences over possessions, you'll find yourself accumulating wealth in the form of cherished memories and enriched relationships rather than redundant belongings. Of course, a key component of financial freedom is effective budgeting and expenditure tracking. Understanding where your money is going empowers you to allocate funds to areas that truly bring value and joy to your life. This conscious approach to spending ensures that your hard-earned cash isn't frittered away, but rather put to work in ways that contribute to your long-term financial independence. In essence, financial freedom is the embodiment of living life without the constraints of monetary concerns. It's about building a secure foundation that affords you the ability to embrace opportunities, weather unexpected storms, and savor the present moment without fretting over the future. As we delve deeper into understanding the dynamics of financial freedom, remember that it's not merely an end goal, but a holistic lifestyle that encompasses mindful decision-making and intentional actions geared towards a liberated and abundant existence.

Building a High-Performing Team

Why It's All About the People

Building a great team starts with understanding that people are your biggest asset. In a world where businesses are obsessed with technology and innovation, it's easy to overlook the fundamental truth: it's the people who make or break a company. Your team is not just a collection of individuals working together; they are the life force that drives your business forward. When you invest in your team, you're investing in the very foundation of your success. But why is it so crucial to prioritize the people side of things? Well, for starters, no amount of cutting-edge technology or groundbreaking ideas can compensate for a team that lacks cohesion, motivation, and passion. Your dream team should be more than just a group of individuals with complementary skills - they should share your vision, embody your values, and bring their own unique strengths to the table. At the end of the day, it's the human connection, the relationships, and the shared sense of purpose that elevate a good team to a truly exceptional one. Building a team that not only gets the job done but also thrives and grows together is an ongoing journey. It's about fostering an environment of trust, empowerment, and open communication. It's about recognizing and nurturing individual talents while also cultivating a collective spirit that propels everyone towards common goals. It's about creating a culture where every member feels valued, heard, and motivated to give their best. So, when you think about assembling your dream team, remember that it's not just about finding the right skill set; it's about finding the right mindset and heart-set. After all, a company is only as strong as the people who power it.

Finding Your Dream Team

So, you're on a quest to find your dream team. It's like putting together the Avengers, but for your business. You want a squad that complements each other's strengths, brings diverse perspectives to the table, and is ready to charge into battle with you. But where to begin? First off, don't just look for clones of yourself – diversity is key! Seek out folks who not only have the skills and experience but also possess that special spark that ignites when they're doing what they love. Consider the kind of personalities that would mesh well with your company culture. Think about the values and work ethic that drive you, and then scout for people who share those same principles. And hey, don't forget to tap into your network. Sometimes, the most unexpected connections can lead you to your next superstar. They might be hiding right under your nose! When it comes to building your dream team, think long-term. Sure, skills are important, but so is potential. Look for individuals who can grow with your company and contribute to its evolution. Don't rush it – finding the perfect fit takes time, like assembling a puzzle where every piece matters. Stay true to your vision, and trust your instincts. The right team is out there, waiting to join you on this epic journey. Get ready to recruit and create your very own band of superheroes.

Crafting a Culture That's Pure Magic

Creating a work culture that's pure magic is like conjuring up the perfect potion – it takes a dash of authenticity, a sprinkle of inclusivity, and a whole lot of intention. It's not just about having a ping-pong table in the break room or offering unlimited snacks (though those are nice perks). A truly magical culture is one where every team member feels valued, supported, and inspired. First off, it starts from the top down. As a leader, you set the tone for the entire team. Your values, actions, and words shape the atmosphere. So, be genuine, communicate openly, and show appreciation for your team's efforts. Encourage creativity and innovation by creating an environment where it's safe to take risks and make mistakes. Next, let's talk about inclusivity. Every person on your team should feel like they belong and that their unique perspective is not only welcomed but celebrated. By fostering a diverse and inclusive environment, you open the doors for fresh ideas, different approaches, and a stronger sense of unity. Consider implementing practices that promote diversity and equity, such as inclusive hiring processes and regular diversity training. Beyond that, recognition is key. Celebrate wins, big or small, and acknowledge the hard work and dedication of each team member. This can be as simple as a shout-out during a team meeting or as grand as an annual awards ceremony. When people feel appreciated, they naturally become more invested in the success of the team. Also, don't forget to nurture a culture of continuous learning and growth. Encourage professional development, provide opportunities for skill-building, and foster mentorship programs. When your team members feel that they're evolving and advancing within the company, they become ambassadors for progress and excellence. Finally, maintain transparency and open lines of communication. This creates trust, reduces misunderstandings, and encourages collaborative problem-solving. Make sure everyone knows that their voice matters and that they have a stake in the company's journey. Crafting a culture that's pure magic isn't a one-time thing; it's an ongoing process. Evaluate periodically, seek feedback from your team, and adapt as necessary. With patience and dedication, you'll create a culture that not only supports your dream team but also propels your business to new heights.

Nailing the Onboarding Process

So, you've found the perfect addition to your dream team—congrats! Now it's time to nail the onboarding process and set them up for success from day one. This initial phase is crucial for integrating new team members into your company culture and ensuring they feel valued and prepared for their role. From paperwork to introductions, here's how to make the onboarding process seamless and impactful. First off, have all the necessary paperwork ready to roll. Make sure your new hire has all employment forms, benefit information, and company policies at their fingertips. Consider creating a welcome package that includes not only these documents but also some fun company swag to instantly make them feel like part of the family. Next, schedule face time with key team members. Set up meetings or casual get-togethers so your new hire can start building relationships with their co-workers. Feeling connected is essential for productivity and overall satisfaction, so encourage open communication and bonding from the get-go. Guide your new team member through an in-depth orientation. This should include a full tour of the office or workspace, a breakdown of the company structure and workflow, and an introduction to any relevant software or tools they'll be using. Providing this comprehensive overview will equip them with the knowledge needed to hit the ground running. Don't forget to establish clear expectations and goals right from the start. Outline their roles and responsibilities, discuss performance expectations, and collaborate on setting achievable, motivating objectives. Creating this roadmap will give them a sense of purpose and direction as they navigate their new role. Finally, check in regularly to receive feedback and address any growing pains. Actively listen to their experiences and thoughts about the onboarding process and beyond. This dialogue will not only help iron out any issues but also showcase that you value their input and are committed to their success within the team. By nailing the onboarding process, you're not only facilitating a smooth transition for your new team member but also laying the foundation for a positive and productive working relationship.

Getting Communication Flowing

You know what makes a high-performing team stand out? Stellar communication. It's like the glue that holds everything together, making sure everyone's on the same page and moving in the same direction. Communication isn't just about talking; it involves listening, understanding, and being open to feedback. So, here's the deal: when you're working with a team, it's crucial to get that communication flowing like a smooth river. First off, transparency is key. Your team should feel comfortable sharing ideas, concerns, and even their latest

Netflix binge without fear of judgment. It's all about creating an environment where everyone feels heard and valued. Next up, embrace different communication styles. Not everyone communicates in the same way. Some folks prefer face-to-face chats, while others thrive on virtual exchanges. By understanding these preferences and adapting your communication methods, you'll ensure that no one gets left out of the loop. And let's not forget about the power of regular check-ins. Whether it's a quick morning huddle or a Friday afternoon catch-up, these moments provide opportunities for sharing wins, discussing challenges, and building camaraderie. Oh, and don't underestimate the magic of non-verbal communication. A supportive nod, a reassuring smile, or even a virtual high-five can speak volumes. Plus, don't be afraid to inject a bit of fun into your interactions. Memes, GIFs, and inside jokes can lighten the mood, strengthen connections, and boost morale. Lastly, consider implementing technology that supports seamless collaboration. From project management platforms to instant messaging apps, there are tons of tools out there that can revolutionize the way your team communicates. By investing in the right tech, you'll streamline processes and foster a more connected work environment. All in all, remember that effective communication isn't just a nice-to-have; it's a must-have for any team aiming for greatness.

Setting Goals Everyone's Excited About

Alright, let's talk about setting goals in a way that gets everyone on board and buzzing with excitement. You know, goals that light up the room and make everyone say, 'Heck yeah, let's do this!' First off, goals need to be crystal clear and inspiring. They should paint a vivid picture of what success looks like for your team, so clear that everyone knows exactly where they're headed and why it matters. No wishy-washy stuff here - we're talking laser-focused targets. But wait, there's more! These goals should be challenging enough to get the adrenaline pumping but still realistic enough to reach. You want that sweet spot where people feel the stretch but not the strain. Now, involving your team in setting these goals is key. Get their input, listen to their ideas, and let them have a hand in shaping the future vision. When people have a say in setting the direction, you can bet they'll be fired up to charge ahead. And don't forget to make these goals measurable and time-bound. It's all about tracking progress and hitting those milestones. When wins start stacking up, motivation levels go through the roof. Lastly, make sure to celebrate every win along the way. Big or small, each victory is a step closer to the finish line. Recognition and rewards keep the energy high and the momentum rolling. With everyone rallied around exciting, achievable goals, your team becomes an unstoppable force, ready to take on anything.

Keeping the Motivation Train on Track

Sometimes, keeping motivation high is like trying to juggle flaming swords while riding a unicycle – challenging but not impossible. As your team navigates the ups and downs of business, it's crucial to keep their fire burning. You might wonder how to maintain that perpetual energy and drive. Well, let's dive into some awesome ways to ensure your squad stays motivated and ready to conquer any challenge. First off, celebrate every little win – big or small, victories are what keep the momentum rolling. Acknowledging their efforts can go a long way in boosting morale and keeping everyone engaged. Next up, create an environment where ideas flow freely. Encourage brainstorming sessions and innovation, and watch those sparks ignite. Another key factor is to be mindful of workload and stress. While pushing boundaries is great, a burned-out team won't produce their best work. Helping them achieve a healthy work-life balance can do wonders for their motivation. Oh, and let's not forget about the power of recognition. Highlighting individual contributions and milestones not only boosts confidence but also inspires others to step up. Incorporating team-building activities is also a win-win. Whether it's a fun outing, volunteering, or just bonding over snacks, these moments can foster strong connections and revitalize team spirits. Lastly, keep the vision alive. Remind them of the bigger picture and how their roles contribute to the organization's success. By painting a compelling future, you're fueling their passion and dedication. Remember, motivation isn't a one-time task; it requires continuous nurturing. So, gear up, sprinkle some positivity, and keep that motivation train chugging along!

Handling Conflicts Like a Pro

Conflict is as inevitable in a team as coffee spills are in a bustling office. It's not about avoiding conflict, but about resolving it like a pro. When tensions arise, address them head-on rather than letting them fester. Encourage open and honest communication, creating a safe space for team members to voice their concerns. But remember, it's not just about calling out the problem; it's also about finding solutions. Approach conflicts with an attitude of problem-solving rather than finger-pointing. Understanding the root cause of the conflict is crucial. Is it a clash of personalities, miscommunication, or differing expectations? Once you identify the underlying issue, work towards a resolution that satisfies all parties involved. Often, conflicts can be opportunities for growth and improvement. Sometimes, it's the clash of ideas that brings about innovation and fresh perspectives. Embrace the diversity of opinions within your team and channel them towards constructive outcomes. When emotions are running high, encourage everyone to take a breather before returning to the discussion. This helps prevent rash decisions and allows for cooler heads to prevail. As a leader, setting an example of grace under pressure can go a long way in diffusing heated situations. It's essential to establish clear protocols for conflict resolution within your team. Define steps for escalating issues and provide resources for mediation if necessary. Lastly, keep an eye out for any recurring patterns in conflicts. Are certain problems arising consistently? If so, there may be deeper systemic issues that need addressing. Remember, mastering conflict resolution takes practice and patience. Cultivate an environment where team members feel heard and respected, and watch as conflicts transform into opportunities for stronger teamwork.

Recognizing and Rewarding Awesomeness

So, let's talk about the fun stuff – recognizing and rewarding awesomeness in your team. When you've got an amazing bunch of people working hard for your business, it's super important to show them some love. Recognition can come in many forms, from a simple shoutout in a team meeting to awards and bonuses. The key is to make sure that everyone feels appreciated for their unique contributions. Remember, not all rewards need to be monetary. Sometimes, a handwritten note or a public acknowledgment can mean the world to someone. It's all about showing genuine appreciation and acknowledging the effort that goes into making your team great. Be creative with your rewards! Maybe it's a monthly

When It's Time to Let Go

Letting go of team members, especially those who have contributed to the growth and success of your business, can be one of the toughest aspects of leadership. But there are times when it becomes necessary for the overall health and productivity of the team and the organization as a whole. Here's how to approach this challenging situation with professionalism and compassion: 1. Continuous Evaluation: Regularly assess each team member's performance and alignment with the company's values and goals. Are they still contributing positively to the team's dynamics and output? Recognize that roles and responsibilities often evolve over time, and what worked at the start may not be suitable in the long run. 2. Open Communication: Create a culture where feedback is actively encouraged and constructively given. If a team member is consistently falling short or causing disruption, address the issues early on. Sometimes, people are unaware of how their behavior impacts others, and providing specific examples can foster understanding and improvement. 3. Identify Root Causes: Is there an underlying reason for the decline in performance or the adverse impact on team morale? Personal struggles, burnout, or a mismatch between the individual and the role can all contribute to subpar performance. A compassionate and open-minded approach to uncovering these reasons is crucial. 4. Support and Development: Before considering letting someone go, explore opportunities for support and development. Training, mentorship, or adjustments to their role might reignite their passion and productivity. However, if these efforts consistently do not yield improvement, it may be time to consider parting ways. 5. Fair Process and Documentation: Be transparent about the process leading up to any decision of dismissal and ensure that it aligns with company policies and legal requirements. Document any performance issues and the steps taken to address them, maintaining thorough records of conversations, warnings, and improvement plans. 6. Compassionate Exit: When the time does come to part ways, approach the situation with empathy and respect. While the conversation may be difficult, be clear and honest about the reasons behind the decision, and offer resources or support to aid in their transition. 7. Team Morale: Acknowledge the potential impact of a team member's departure on the rest of the team. Communicate openly, reassuring the team of the organization's commitment to their wellbeing and the steps being taken to maintain productivity and cohesiveness. Remember, letting go of team members is a natural part of business evolution, however difficult it may be. By approaching these situations with care and diligence, you can uphold the integrity of your team and pave the way for new opportunities and growth.

Strategic Marketing and Sales

Setting the Stage: Why Marketing and Sales Matter

Understanding the core reasons behind your marketing and sales tactics is crucial for aligning your efforts with business goals. Marketing and sales are like the dynamic duo of your business, working together to achieve one common objective: driving growth. Without effective marketing and sales strategies, even the most groundbreaking products or services may struggle to gain traction in the market. So, why do they matter? For starters, marketing is all about creating awareness and interest in what you have to offer. It's your chance to showcase the value and benefits of your product or service in a compelling and irresistible way. This is the stage where you get to tell your story and make people sit up and take notice. On the other hand, sales is the engine that drives revenue and sustains your business. It's all well and good to have an amazing product, but without sales, it's just a well-kept secret. Your sales efforts are the bridge between your offering and your customers – they turn interest and curiosity into tangible business results. More than just driving revenue, though, marketing and sales provide valuable insights into market trends, customer behavior, and the competitive landscape. By understanding the needs and preferences of your audience, you can tailor your offerings to meet those needs and stand out from the competition. In essence, effective marketing and sales efforts are essential for not only attracting new customers but also retaining existing ones. They help build brand loyalty and advocacy, turning one-time buyers into repeat customers and advocates for your brand. Moreover, they play a critical role in differentiating your business from the competition and carving out a unique position in the market. Ultimately, by integrating marketing and sales into your overall business strategy, you can establish a strong foundation for sustained growth and success.

Knowing Your Audience: Who Are We Talking To?

So, you want to knock the socks off your audience, right? Well, first things first: you need to know who they are. I'm not just talking demographics here, although age, gender, location, and all that jazz do matter. What's really important is understanding their hopes, dreams, fears, and pain points. Think about it—when was the last time you truly connected with someone who didn't get you? Yeah, that's what I thought. Your audience is no different. Whether you're selling organic granola or high-tech gadgets, you've got to get inside their heads. How? Ask yourself: What keeps them up at night? What makes them jump for joy? What gets them riled up? Once you've answered those questions, you'll start to see patterns emerge, and that's where the magic happens. You'll uncover the language, imagery, and messaging that resonates with your peeps. You might even find that quirky meme or heartfelt story that tugs at their heartstrings. The more you understand your audience, the easier it becomes to create marketing and sales strategies that hit the bullseye. Now, I'm not saying it's a walk in the park. It takes time, research, and a whole lot of empathy. But trust me, once you get a handle on who your audience really is, you'll wonder how you ever did business without this insight. So, grab a cuppa, put yourself in their shoes, and get ready to speak their language like never before.

Crafting Your Message: What's the Story?

Okay, so you know who your audience is now. Great! But how do you speak their language? How do you tell a story that resonates with them? Crafting your message isn't just about throwing words together; it's about creating a narrative that connects with people on a deeper level. First things first, you have to understand what makes your audience tick. What are their pain points, desires, and values? Dive deep into their world and figure out what matters to them. Once you've got a good handle on that, it's time to shape your message. Your story should be authentic and relatable. No one likes a phony, so be real. Share your own experiences, struggles, and triumphs. Let people see the humanity behind your brand. It's about building trust and establishing a genuine connection. But hey, it's not all about you. Your story also needs to show how you can make your audience's lives better. What problem can you solve for them? How can you add value? Your message should be all about them, not just singing your own praises. And let's talk about the medium. Are you using social media, email, videos, or all of the above? Each platform has its own vibe, so tailor your message to fit. A snappy tweet might not work as an in-depth blog post, and vice versa. Mix it up, stay consistent, but always keep your audience in mind. Now, visuals. People love pictures, so don't skimp on the graphics. Whether it's a stunning Instagram photo, an eye-catching infographic, or a well-designed logo, visuals can really elevate your storytelling game. Remember, your message isn't set in stone. It's okay to experiment, tweak, and refine. Get feedback, see what resonates, and adjust accordingly. The best stories evolve over time, so don't shy away from making changes. In the end, crafting your message is about creating a narrative that captivates, inspires, and drives action. It's your chance to spark emotion, create connection, and leave a lasting impression. So go ahead, find your voice, and tell a story that truly speaks to your audience.

Choosing the Right Channels: Where's the Party?

Alright, so you've got your message down pat. It's compelling, it's on point, and it's ready to rock the world. But hold up a sec—where are you planning to showcase this masterpiece? That's where choosing the right channels comes into play. Think of it like this—you wouldn't host a wild beach party in the middle of the city, right? You'd head to the coast for that. In the same way, you need to find the perfect 'party spot' for your message. Maybe it's social media, perhaps it's email marketing, or even good old-fashioned face-to-face networking. Each channel has its own vibe and audience, so you want to go where your peeps hang out. Do some research, look at where your competitors are making waves, and figure out which platforms make the most sense for your business. Remember, it's not just about being present—it's about being present where it matters. So, grab your party hat and get ready to join the shindig on the channels that truly align with your brand and your audience. Let's get this party started!

Building Relationships: It's Not All About the Sale

When it comes to business, it can be tempting to focus solely on the sale. After all, that's the ultimate goal, right? Well, not quite. Building strong and meaningful relationships with your customers is what sets apart a successful business from the rest. It's about creating a connection that goes beyond the transaction. Think of it as planting seeds that will grow into loyal customers and advocates for your brand. But how do you do that? First off, listen to your customers. Really listen. Understand their needs, their challenges, and their goals. Show genuine interest in their success, and they'll return the favor by trusting and valuing your expertise. Next, be authentic. People can sniff out insincerity from a mile away. So, be real with your customers. Share your story, your values, and the passion behind what you do. This authenticity will resonate with them and lay the foundation for a lasting relationship. Don't forget to add value without expecting anything in return. Provide helpful resources, tips, and advice that genuinely benefit your customers, even if it doesn't lead directly to a sale. This demonstrates your commitment to their success and fosters a sense of reciprocity. Remember, building relationships takes time, effort, and consistency. Stay in touch, follow up, and show gratitude. A simple thank-you note can go a long way. Lastly, admit when you mess up. No one's perfect, and acknowledging mistakes and working to make things right builds trust and credibility. By focusing on building relationships, not just making sales, you'll cultivate a community of loyal supporters who believe in your brand and are eager to spread the word. In the end, it's these genuine connections that will drive sustainable success for your business.

Sales Strategies That Don't Suck

Alright, let's talk about sales strategies that actually work without making you feel like a sleazy used car salesman. The key here is authenticity. People can smell a phony sales pitch from miles away, so it's important to approach sales with honesty and integrity. First off, focus on building trust. You want your customers to feel confident that you genuinely have their best interests at heart. This means listening to their needs, providing valuable solutions, and being transparent about what you're offering. Nobody likes a pushy salesperson, so take a chill pill and let the process unfold naturally. Next, find ways to add value before asking for the sale. This could be through sharing helpful resources, offering free trials, or providing exceptional customer service. When you demonstrate your commitment to adding value, people are more likely to reciprocate with their business. Another killer sales strategy is storytelling. People connect with stories, so weave a narrative that showcases how your product or service has positively impacted others. This allows potential customers to see themselves in the story and understand the real-world benefits of what you're offering. Now, let's talk about the power of relationship-building. Sales isn't just about closing deals; it's about cultivating long-term relationships. Stay in touch with your customers, show appreciation for their business, and continue providing support even after the sale. This will result in loyal customers who not only come back for more but also become powerful advocates for your brand. Lastly, embrace the art of the follow-up. Sometimes, the timing just isn't right for a potential customer, so don't be afraid to check in periodically to see if their situation has changed. A friendly email or call to touch base can make all the difference. Remember, the goal is to stay top-of-mind without being annoying. Alright, those are some solid sales strategies that won't make you cringe. Let's move on to turning feedback into gold!

Turning Feedback into Gold

Alright, so you've made some sales and hopefully received some feedback from your customers. Now, it's time to turn that feedback into gold. Customer feedback is like a treasure trove of insights that can help you improve your products or services, tailor your marketing and sales strategies, and ultimately build stronger relationships with your audience. First off, take all the feedback with a grain of salt. Not everyone will have constructive criticism, and that's okay. But for those nuggets of wisdom in there, make sure to listen attentively. One of the first things you'll want to do is categorize the feedback. Are there recurring themes or patterns? This could be gold dust when it comes to identifying areas for improvement or features to emphasize in your marketing. Next, don't just stop at listening - engage with your customers about their feedback. They'll appreciate the fact that you're actively seeking their input, and you may uncover even more valuable insights in the process. Now, let's talk about turning this feedback into action. Maybe there are specific pain points that customers keep mentioning - dive into these and see if there are effective solutions you can implement. If customers are raving about certain aspects of your product or service, find ways to amplify that in your messaging and promotions. Of course, it's not just about what customers say directly to you. Keep an eye on social media, online reviews, and any other public platforms where people are talking about your brand. Address negative feedback gracefully, and use it as an opportunity to showcase your dedication to customer satisfaction. When it comes to positive feedback, share it proudly! Testimonials and success stories can be pure gold when it comes to building trust with potential customers. Finally, remember that feedback is an ongoing resource. Regularly revisit and reassess the feedback you've received, as your business evolves, so should your listening strategy. So, there you have it - turning feedback into gold doesn't happen overnight, but it's an essential part of building a successful and customer-focused business. Take the time to listen, engage, and take action, and you'll be well on your way to striking gold in the world of marketing and sales.

Tools of the Trade: Must-Have Tech and Tools

When it comes to strategic marketing and sales, having the right tools at your disposal can make all the difference. In today's digital age, there is a plethora of tech and tools designed to streamline processes, analyze data, and improve efficiency in reaching your audience. Let's dive into some of the must-have assets that every savvy marketer and sales professional should consider incorporating into their arsenal. First and foremost, a robust customer relationship management (CRM) software is essential for keeping track of leads, managing contacts, and nurturing relationships. This type of platform allows you to collect and analyze valuable customer data, providing insights that can inform your marketing and sales strategies. Additionally, email marketing automation tools can help you create and send targeted, personalized communications at scale, saving time and ensuring consistency. Social media management platforms are also invaluable, offering powerful scheduling, monitoring, and analytical capabilities across various channels. These tools empower you to engage with your audience, measure performance, and adapt your approach as needed. When it comes to sales, having a reliable sales enablement platform can enhance productivity and collaboration among your sales team, providing access to content, training materials, and customer insights. Furthermore, integrating analytics tools such as Google Analytics or similar offerings can provide valuable insights into website traffic, user behavior, and campaign performance. By leveraging these insights, you can optimize your marketing activities and tailor your messaging to resonate with your audience. The beauty of technology is its potential to continually evolve and improve business practices. As the marketing and sales landscape continues to shift, staying updated on emerging technologies and trends is crucial. Exploring new tools, attending industry events, and networking with peers can expose you to innovative solutions that could give your business a competitive edge. Ultimately, investing in the right tech and tools not only streamlines your processes but also empowers you to make informed decisions based on real-time data.

Whether it's harnessing the power of AI-driven analytics or utilizing intuitive marketing automation platforms, equipping yourself with the latest tools can transform the way you engage with your audience and drive sales. As we navigate the digital frontier, being adaptable and proactive in integrating these resources will set you apart from the pack and position your business for sustained success.

Measuring Success: What Do the Numbers Say?

Alright, folks, it's time to get down to the nitty-gritty and talk about measuring success. In the world of marketing and sales, numbers are our best friends and our harshest critics. We need to know what's working, what's not, and where we can make improvements. So, let's dive into the metrics that matter. First up, we've got to look at the basics. How many leads are coming in? What's our conversion rate? These are the foundational numbers that give us a sense of how well our efforts are paying off. But we can't stop there. We need to dig deeper. What's the customer acquisition cost? Are our marketing campaigns bringing in qualified leads, or are we just casting a wide net? Then there's the ever-important question of engagement. How are people interacting with our content? Are they clicking, sharing, and commenting? These actions tell us if we're striking a chord with our audience or missing the mark. And let's not forget about website analytics. Where are people dropping off? What pages are generating the most interest? This data guides us in optimizing our online presence for maximum impact. But wait, there's more! Sales numbers paint a picture of their own. Are we hitting our revenue targets? What's the average deal size? Are there any patterns in the sales cycle that we can capitalize on? And speaking of patterns, let's not overlook the power of trend analysis. Are there seasonal trends that influence our sales? What about shifts in customer behavior? Of course, it's not all about the quantitative data. Qualitative feedback is equally valuable. What are customers saying about us? Are there recurring themes in their feedback? What do they love about our products or services, and where do they feel we could improve? These insights help us shape our offerings to better meet customer needs. Now, I know what you're thinking – this all sounds like a lot of work. And you're not wrong. Measuring success can be a hefty task, but it's absolutely essential. Without understanding the numbers, we're just shooting in the dark. So, let's roll up our sleeves, dive into the data, and use it to steer our marketing and sales efforts toward even greater success.

Lessons Learned: Reflections from the Trenches

All right, folks, gather around because it's storytelling time. When it comes to navigating the marketing and sales landscape, there's no teacher quite as potent as experience. We've all been there, hustling to crack the code, trying different approaches, and learning through trial and error. Today, I want to share with you some of the hard-earned lessons and insights gathered by individuals who have ventured into the trenches of marketing and sales. These tales aren't just about wins and losses; they're about uncovering the hidden gems in the rough. One thing that stands out is the importance of staying adaptable. Markets shift, customer preferences evolve, and what worked yesterday might not cut it tomorrow. It's crucial to embrace change and be open to refining your strategies. Many seasoned entrepreneurs emphasize the significance of building authentic relationships. Beyond the numbers and bottom line, it's the trust and rapport you establish with your audience that can make or break your brand. Customers want to feel valued, heard, and understood, and that takes more than a flashy ad campaign. As we delve deeper, we encounter stories of resilience. Success rarely happens overnight, and setbacks are inevitable. What sets apart the best from the rest is their ability to bounce back and extract wisdom from adversity. These reflections underscore the need for patience and perseverance. Innovation is another recurring theme. Those who stand out often broke the mold and did things differently. They discovered innovative ways to reach their audience, whether through unconventional marketing channels or revolutionary sales techniques. In this fast-paced digital age, creativity and originality are prized more than ever. Moreover, the idea of continuous learning resonates strongly. The veterans speak of how they never stopped seeking knowledge and honing their craft. Whether it's keeping up with industry trends, attending workshops, or networking with like-minded professionals, ongoing education is fundamental. Lastly, the spirit of humility and empathy emerges. No one has all the answers, and everyone's journey is unique. The most successful individuals remain humble, open to feedback, and eager to learn from others. Empathy for the customer's perspective is also a tenet many swear by, understanding that behind every sale is a human story. So, as we wrap up these reflections from the front lines, remember that these lessons are not just words on a page; they're the crux of what it means to thrive in the world of marketing and sales.

Scaling Sustainably

Intro: Why Scaling Isn't Just About Getting Bigger

Sometimes the desire to scale can overshadow critical business needs. Many entrepreneurs equate growth with success, and while expansion is undoubtedly essential, it's vital to approach it strategically. Scaling isn't just about getting bigger; it's about enriching your impact, securing long-term sustainability, and enhancing the value you deliver to your customers. So, when crafting your vision for growth, it's crucial to think beyond mere numbers. Consider how your business can foster meaningful connections, innovate in its sector, and contribute positively to the lives of those it reaches. Your vision should encompass not only quantitative milestones but also qualitative aspects that reflect your values and aspirations. How do you want your company to be perceived by both employees and customers as it scales? What legacy do you hope to leave in your industry or community? These questions are essential in sculpting a vision that goes beyond the traditional metrics of growth. They guide you in building a company that aligns with your purpose and resonates deeply with your audience. Remember that creating a vision for growth isn't solely a solitary endeavor. Seek input from your team, partners, mentors, and even customers. Their diverse perspectives can help shape a more comprehensive and realistic vision, one that acknowledges the potential challenges and opportunities ahead. Ultimately, a compelling vision for growth serves as a beacon, guiding your decisions and actions as your business evolves. It's the compass that keeps you aligned with your core values and purpose, anchoring your scaling efforts in a holistic, sustainable approach.

Creating a Vision for Growth

So, you've realized that scaling your business isn't just about getting bigger - it's about ensuring sustainable growth and maintaining what makes your company special. Now, let's talk about one of the most crucial aspects of this process: creating a vision for growth. It's like mapping out the route for a road trip – without a clear destination in mind, you could end up anywhere. Your vision serves as the north star that guides every decision and effort toward the future. So, how do you go about crafting this vision? First things first, envision what success looks like for your business in the next 5, 10, or even 20 years. Get specific and paint a vivid picture of where you see your company. Consider factors like revenue, market share, geographical reach, and even the impact you want to make on the world. Keep in mind that your vision should also resonate with your team and customers, reflecting the values and mission that set your company apart. It's not just about numbers; it's about weaving a compelling narrative that inspires everyone involved. Once you have this overarching vision, break it down into measurable milestones. Think of these as pit stops along the road to success – they help you track progress and ensure you're staying on course. These could include reaching certain revenue targets, expanding into new markets, or launching innovative products. Align these milestones with your company's overall purpose and values, making sure they contribute meaningfully to the larger vision. Lastly, communicate this vision effectively throughout your organization. Make it part of your company culture, infusing it into everything from team meetings to performance reviews. The more your team internalizes this vision, the more empowered and aligned they'll be in driving the business forward. Remember, the journey of scaling sustainably isn't just about the destination; it's about the experiences and impact you create along the way.

Balancing Speed and Stability

So, you've got this amazing vision for your business growth, and now comes the tricky part – finding that perfect balance between speed and stability. Sure, you want to scale up quickly and make a big impact, but rushing too fast can lead to shaky foundations and potential burnout. On the flip side, being overly cautious might result in missed opportunities and stagnation. It's like walking on a tightrope – one step too brisk, and you could lose your footing; one step too tentative, and you won't get anywhere at all. Let's talk about speed. Yes, it's tempting to race towards expansion, especially when you see other businesses skyrocketing seemingly overnight. But hold on a minute! How about we take a look at creating sustainable growth instead? After all, building a sturdy ladder one careful step at a time is often a smarter move than trying to leap up the entire staircase in one go! Stability is the cornerstone of successful scaling. It involves putting down solid roots before shooting upwards, ensuring that each level of growth is supported by a robust foundation. This means having the right systems and processes in place to handle the increased demand while maintaining the quality that your customers expect. It's about taking the time to build trust and reliability, rather than just chasing after the next big thing. Balance becomes crucial here. Finding the equilibrium between speed and stability requires thoughtful planning and strategic decision-making. You'll need to assess the risks and rewards of each move, understanding that sometimes, slow and steady truly does win the race. But don't worry; it doesn't mean you have to grind to a halt – it's more about pacing yourself and recognizing when to press the accelerator and when to ease off. Remember, successful scaling isn't just about reaching the finish line; it's also about staying there and flourishing once you do. So, think of it as a marathon, not a sprint. Pace yourself, keep your eyes on the prize, and savor every stride forward. The journey itself is just as important as the destination, if not more so. By striking a harmonious balance between speed and stability, you'll set your business up for sustainable, long-lasting success – and that's a race worth running.

People Power: Hiring the Right Team

Building the right team is like crafting a winning recipe – you need the perfect blend of ingredients. Every member brings a unique flavor to the mix, and when combined, their skills, personalities, and work ethics create a delicious synergy that propels your business forward. But how do you find these outstanding team players? First things first, it's not just about the resumes. Sure, qualifications matter, but it's equally essential to look beyond paper credentials. You want individuals who fit into your company culture, share your ethos, and bring diverse perspectives to the table. Building a diverse team isn't just a buzzword; it's key to innovation and problem-solving. So, tap into networks beyond the traditional hiring grounds. Seek out talent from various backgrounds and experiences. Look for those who not only have the required skills but also showcase adaptability and a thirst for continuous learning. The interview process holds immense power. It's akin to meeting a potential new friend – you're not just assessing skills; you're gauging how well they'll gel with your existing crew. Engage them in conversations that dig deeper than work history. Ask about their passions, their favorite activities outside of work, and what drives them. Understanding their motivations and seeing how they communicate can be telling. And don't stop with the interviews. Rely on references and recommendations from people whose opinions you value. When you've found your star players, support them with ample resources and meaningful feedback. Encourage an environment where open communication and constructive criticism are not just tolerated but celebrated. Build an atmosphere where everyone feels valued and has room to grow. Remember, hiring is only half the battle. Once you have your dream team assembled, invest in team building activities and nurture a positive work culture. Host regular check-ins to understand their aspirations and challenges. Recognize their efforts and celebrate their victories. By laying the foundation for trust and camaraderie, you're building a team that's not just working for you, but with you, towards a common goal. Because a strong team isn't just a group of individuals – it's a dynamic force that drives your business towards success.

Tech and Tools: Smart Investments for Expansion

So, you've got the dream team in place, and your business is ready to take the next big step. But how can you ensure that this growth is not just expansion for expansion's sake, but a strategic, sustainable progression? That's where smart investments in technology and tools come into play. In today's fast-paced digital landscape, leveraging the right tech can be a game-changer for businesses looking to scale effectively. First off, it's crucial to assess your current workflow and identify pain points that could be addressed with technological solutions. Whether it's streamlining communication, optimizing project management, or automating repetitive tasks, there's an array of software and tools designed to make your operations more efficient. From project management platforms like Asana and Trello to customer relationship management (CRM) systems such as Salesforce or HubSpot, there's no shortage of options to explore. Beyond internal processes, investing in robust cybersecurity measures is non-negotiable. As your business grows, so does the value of the data you hold, making you a more attractive target for cyber threats. Implementing firewalls, encryption, and regular security audits can safeguard your company against potential breaches and data loss, earning the trust of both customers and stakeholders. Moreover, as your customer base expands, embracing technology to enhance the customer experience becomes paramount. This could mean integrating a seamless e-commerce platform, developing a user-friendly mobile app, or leveraging data analytics to personalize marketing campaigns. The key here is to invest in tools that not only cater to your current needs but also have the scalability to support your future growth. When it comes to financial investment, it's essential to strike a balance between cost and long-term benefits. While cutting-edge technologies may seem appealing, consider their ROI and whether they align with your overarching goals. It's often wiser to start with scalable, modular solutions that can adapt as your business evolves, rather than sinking excessive funds into complex systems with limited flexibility. Lastly, don't underestimate the power of ongoing education and training for your team to maximize the potential of these new tools. Investing in workshops, online courses, or specialized certifications can equip your employees with the skills needed to leverage these technologies effectively, ensuring that your tech investments translate into tangible results. In a nutshell, the right tech and tools can propel your business to new heights, but it's vital to approach these investments with a discerning eye. By strategically leveraging technology, you're not just setting your business up for expansion; you're fortifying its foundation for sustainable, long-term success.

Crafting a Scalable Business Model

Creating a scalable business model is like building a sturdy foundation for a skyscraper. It's not just about reaching greater heights quickly; it's about ensuring that as you grow, everything remains structurally sound and sustainable. So, what goes into crafting such a model? Let's dig in. First off, your scalability hinges on having a value proposition that can withstand the test of growth. This means offering something that customers consistently find valuable, even as your business expands. It's all about finding that sweet spot where demand for your offering can increase without escalating costs at the same rate. Next up, processes and systems need to be streamlined and flexible. You want to pave the way for growth without causing unnecessary bottlenecks or chaos. Technology plays a massive role here—one that's more important than ever in our digital age. By leveraging the right tools, automation, and data-driven insights, you're effectively laying down the tracks for smooth expansion. Another critical aspect is understanding your target market and how it might evolve. What works for your current audience may not always work for a larger, more diverse customer base. This calls for strategic foresight and adaptability. As you scale, you'll also need to keep a close eye on your operational costs and revenue streams. The goal isn't just to grow, but to do so profitably. Here's where financial acumen comes into play, helping you make informed decisions that support your long-term vision. Lastly, a truly scalable business model fosters a culture of innovation and continuous improvement. It's about embracing change, being open to new ideas, and learning from both successes and failures. This mindset permeates throughout the organization, driving creativity and resilience. Crafting a scalable business model isn't a one-size-fits-all endeavor. It requires a deep understanding of your industry, market dynamics, and internal capabilities. But when done right, it paves the way for sustainable, impactful growth that stands the test of time.

Financial Foundations for Growth

Alright, let's dive into the nitty-gritty of financial foundations for your business's growth. We're talking about more than just balancing the books here – we're getting into the nuts and bolts of setting your business up for long-term success. First off, it's crucial to have a solid financial plan in place. That means keeping track of your cash flow, managing expenses, and projecting revenue. You want to be able to see where your money is coming from and where it's going at all times. This way, you can make informed decisions about where to invest and how to allocate resources for growth. Speaking of investment, don't overlook the importance of financial discipline. It can be tempting to splurge when you start seeing some success, but maintaining financial discipline is key to sustained growth. This might mean making strategic choices about when and where to spend your hard-earned cash. Think of it as laying the groundwork for future expansion. And let's not forget about funding. As you scale your business, you may find that you need additional capital to fuel your growth. Whether it's through loans, investors, or other means, having a clear plan for securing funding will be essential. It's also important to keep an eye on your credit and financial relationships to ensure you maintain access to the resources you need. Finally, risk management plays a huge role in establishing financial foundations for growth. Understanding and mitigating potential risks – whether they're related to market fluctuations, regulatory changes, or other factors – is key to protecting the financial health of your business as it grows. By being proactive and adaptable, you can build resilience into your financial strategy and prepare for whatever the future holds. Remember, a strong financial foundation is the bedrock of sustainable growth, so take the time to get it right.

Gazing into the Crystal Ball: Forecasting and Adapting

Alright, so you've got a vision for where you want your business to go, and you've laid down some solid financial groundwork. Now it's time to bust out the crystal ball and start peering into the future. We're not talking about making wild guesses here. No, we're diving deep into forecasting and adapting – the keys to staying ahead of the game. Let's break it down. First off, forecasting. This isn't just about looking at sales numbers and hoping for the best. It's about using past data, industry trends, and market analysis to paint a clear picture of what lies ahead. You'll want to crunch those numbers, but also trust your instincts. Understanding the potential challenges and opportunities that may come your way is crucial. With solid forecasting in place, you can better prepare your business for whatever the future throws at it. But hey, we all know that things don't always go according to plan, right? That's where adapting comes in. Flexibility is your friend when it comes to scaling sustainably. Your forecast might not always pan out, and that's okay. Being able to pivot, adjust strategies, and embrace change is what sets successful businesses apart. Keep your finger on the pulse of market shifts and consumer behavior. Stay nimble and open to new ideas. Sometimes, the best opportunities are hidden in the wrinkles of unexpected changes. The key is to remain agile and ready to shift gears when necessary. So, as you look into that figurative crystal ball, remember that the future is not set in stone. It's a landscape waiting to be shaped by your decisions and actions. Embrace the uncertainty with a sense of adventure. Foresee, adapt, and steer your business toward sustainable growth – one step at a time.

The Environmental Impact of Scaling

When we talk about scaling a business, we often focus on growth, profits, and expansion. However, it's crucial to consider the environmental impact of this expansion. As your business grows, so do its resource needs and waste production, which can have significant implications for the environment. One major environmental consideration when scaling is your energy consumption. With an increase in operations, your energy demands will likely rise. It's essential to assess how your business can minimize its energy usage through efficiency measures, renewable energy sources, and responsible consumption practices. Another critical factor to address is the carbon footprint of your scaling activities. Whether it's increased transportation for product distribution or a larger physical footprint for facilities, every expansion comes with potential emissions. To mitigate this, businesses should explore sustainable transportation options, adopt green building practices, and prioritize eco-friendly supply chain logistics. Water usage is also a concern when scaling a business. As your operations grow, so does your demand for water, which can strain local water supplies and ecosystems. Implementing water-efficient technologies, recycling water where possible, and supporting community water conservation efforts are meaningful steps in reducing your business's water footprint. Waste management becomes more complex as a company scales. Increased production often means increased waste generation. Taking proactive measures to minimize waste, recycle materials, and incorporate circular economy principles into your business model can significantly reduce the environmental impact of your growth. Furthermore, scaling can have indirect ecological effects, such as habitat destruction, deforestation, and biodiversity loss due to land development or sourcing practices. Sustainable sourcing, reforestation initiatives, and fostering partnerships with conservation organizations can help offset these impacts. Finally, it's important for businesses to engage with their stakeholders and local communities to understand and address any environmental concerns associated with their scaling initiatives. By fostering open dialogue and collaboration, companies can work towards minimizing their environmental footprint and contributing positively to the communities in which they operate. Considering the environmental impact of scaling isn't just about being a responsible corporate citizen; it's also about ensuring the long-term sustainability of your business. Embracing environmentally conscious practices during the scaling process can lead to cost savings, operational efficiencies, and enhanced brand reputation. Ultimately, by prioritizing the planet while growing your business, you can create a positive legacy that extends far beyond the bottom line.

Wrap Up: Keeping Your Identity as You Grow

When scaling your business, it's easy to lose sight of the core values and unique identity that set you apart in the first place. As you embark on the journey of growth, it's crucial to remember where you came from and what makes your brand special. One of the biggest challenges in this process is maintaining the authenticity and culture that defined your company from the beginning. It's about staying true to your roots while adapting to new opportunities and challenges. Your identity is not just a logo or a tagline; it's the essence of what makes your business unique. It's the stories you tell, the way you treat your customers, and the values that drive every decision. As you scale, it's important to keep this identity at the forefront of everything you do. We've all seen businesses lose their identity as they chase rapid growth, leading to a loss of trust and connection with their audience. To avoid this pitfall, consider how your growth strategy aligns with the core elements of your brand. Communicate these elements clearly to your team so that everyone understands and embodies the essence of your company. Remember to celebrate milestones and victories in a way that reflects your brand's personality. Whether it's a small team lunch or a grand event, let your culture shine through. At the same time, always be open to evolution and change. As your business expands, your identity will naturally evolve. Embrace this transformation while staying grounded in the values that have brought you success. Finally, never underestimate the power of storytelling. Use your brand's narrative to connect with customers, employees, and partners on a deeper level. Share the ups and downs of your journey, the lessons learned, and the vision for the future. By weaving these stories into your growth strategy, you'll create an emotional bond that transcends scale. In the end, the key to keeping your identity intact as you grow is to make it a conscious priority. It's not something that happens by chance; it requires intentional effort and constant evaluation. With each decision and action, ask yourself if it aligns with the heart and soul of your brand. This mindful approach will ensure that your growth journey not only brings success but also preserves the magic that made your business special in the first place.

Setting Boundaries and Saying No

Why Boundaries Matter: Keeping Your Sanity

Setting clear boundaries isn't just about asserting control over your time and energy; it's about safeguarding your mental well-being. Imagine constantly saying 'yes' to every request that comes your way, whether it's from clients, colleagues, or friends. The result? You'd find yourself stretched thin, juggling an avalanche of responsibilities with no time left for yourself. It's a fast track to burnout, both physically and mentally. Without defined boundaries, you risk becoming overwhelmed, stressed, and ultimately unable to perform at your best. Recognizing the signs of burnout early on is crucial. It could manifest as constant fatigue, decreased motivation, or feeling detached from your work and personal life. By understanding the personal impacts of not setting clear boundaries, you'll gain insight into how protecting your time and resources can directly influence your overall well-being. Picture this: instead of frantically trying to keep up with an ever-expanding to-do list, you have the freedom to pursue activities that recharge your batteries and bring joy to your life. Setting boundaries isn't selfish; it's an act of self-preservation, ensuring you're able to show up as the best version of yourself in all aspects of your life.

Spotting the Signs: When You're Overwhelmed

We've all been there, haven't we? That feeling of constant overwhelm that seems to creep into every corner of our lives. It's like trying to juggle a dozen balls at once, and no matter how hard you try, they just keep slipping through your fingers. But here's the thing – overwhelm doesn't just happen out of the blue. There are always signs, clues, little whispers from your body and mind that say, 'Hey, maybe slow down a bit.' So, let's tune in and listen to what those signs might be. One of the most common indicators of overwhelm is physical fatigue. When you find yourself constantly tired, achy, or just lacking energy, it could be your body's way of telling you to ease up. Pay attention to those recurring headaches, tense muscles, or even an upset stomach – these are all red flags that your body is under too much stress. Then there's the mental side of things. When your brain feels like a tangled mess of thoughts and worries, it's a good sign that overwhelm is lurking nearby. You might notice an increase in forgetfulness, difficulty concentrating, or racing thoughts that just won't quit. Emotional cues can also clue you into overwhelm. Feeling irritable, on edge, or overly emotional for no apparent reason could be your emotions signaling for a breather. Lastly, pay attention to your behavior. Are you withdrawing from social activities, neglecting self-care, or finding it challenging to make even the smallest decisions? These are all signs that overwhelm has taken hold. The key is to recognize these signals early on and take proactive steps to address them. In the next section, we'll delve into the power of saying no and how it can be a game-changer in reclaiming your sense of calm and balance.

The Power of No: Not a Dirty Word

So, you're probably familiar with the feeling of wanting to please everyone and saying yes to everything that comes your way. The thing is, it's impossible to do it all without sacrificing your own well-being. That's where the power of 'no' comes in. It's not about being selfish or uncaring; it's about setting healthy boundaries and honoring your own needs. When you say no to something, you're actually saying yes to yourself. You're prioritizing what truly matters to you. It's a form of self-respect, and it's essential for maintaining balance in both your personal and professional life. Saying no allows you to focus on the things that align with your goals and values. It gives you the freedom to dedicate your time and energy to activities that bring you fulfillment and joy. Let's face it, if you say yes to everything, you'll end up burnt out and resentful. Learning to say no with confidence and grace is a skill that will serve you well in various aspects of your life. Whether it's declining an extra project at work when your plate is already full or politely turning down social invitations when you need some downtime, the power of 'no' empowers you to take control of your time and commitments. However, it's important to acknowledge that saying no can be challenging, especially if you're used to being a people-pleaser. You might fear disappointing others or feel guilty for turning down opportunities. But remember, it's okay to prioritize your own well-being. Finding a balance between giving and preserving your own resources is key to living a fulfilling and sustainable life. So, embrace the power of 'no' as a tool for taking care of yourself and creating space for the things that truly matter to you.

Finding Your 'Yes': Knowing What You Truly Want

We've all been told that saying 'no' is important, but have you ever thought about what you're really saying 'yes' to? It's time to hone in on what truly matters to you. Everybody has their own unique set of values and desires, and it's crucial to recognize and honor those. Identifying your 'yes' means taking a deep dive into your innermost aspirations and convictions. What are the things that light a fire within you? What makes you feel alive and purposeful? Reflecting on these questions can lead you to discover the core essence of your 'yes'. Maybe it's pursuing a creative passion, building meaningful relationships, or striving for personal growth. Whatever it may be, don't let external pressures dictate your 'yes'. Once you unearth your 'yes', embrace it wholeheartedly and integrate it into your decision-making process. At times, this might call for saying 'no' to opportunities that don't align with your true desires and values. It's about understanding that every 'no' you utter is clearing the path for a resounding 'yes' to the things that resonate with your soul. This journey of discovery isn't about limiting yourself; it's about empowering yourself to live authentically and passionately. As you navigate through the process of finding your 'yes', remember that it's an evolving and dynamic adventure. Embrace the twists and turns, the highs and lows, and allow your 'yes' to guide you towards a life infused with purpose, fulfillment, and joy.

Communicating Boundaries Like a Pro

Setting boundaries is vital for maintaining your well-being, but communicating them effectively can be a game-changer. When it comes to expressing your boundaries, clarity is key. Use assertive yet respectful language to convey your needs and limits. Be direct and specific about what you are comfortable with and what crosses the line. Remember, setting boundaries is not about being aggressive; it's about honoring your own needs and maintaining healthy relationships. It's important to communicate your boundaries in a timely manner. Waiting until you're on the verge of frustration or resentment can lead to unnecessary tension. Choose an appropriate time and place to have these conversations, ensuring that both parties are receptive and focused. Frame your boundaries as a means of nurturing the relationship rather than creating distance. Consider using

Handling Pushback with Grace

So, you've set your boundaries like a pro, but what happens when others push back? Dealing with pushback is often the most challenging part of establishing and maintaining healthy boundaries. It's natural for people to test limits or express discomfort when faced with change. However, handling pushback with grace can reinforce your boundaries and strengthen your relationships. First and foremost, it's crucial to approach pushback with empathy and understanding. Try to see things from the other person's perspective. Their resistance might stem from their own insecurities or fear of change. By acknowledging their concerns, you demonstrate that you value their feelings and opinions. Additionally, maintaining a calm and composed demeanor during these interactions can help diffuse tension and create a conducive environment for constructive dialogue. When facing pushback, effective communication plays a pivotal role. Clearly articulating your reasons for establishing boundaries and the positive impact they have on both parties can provide much-needed context. Listening actively to the concerns raised by the other party and addressing them with respect can foster mutual understanding. Acknowledge their perspectives, and if necessary, make adjustments to the boundaries in a way that aligns with both parties' needs. It's equally important to remain firm in upholding your boundaries while being open to compromise where reasonable. This balance demonstrates assertiveness without being rigid. Remember, the goal is not to shut others out, but to create a healthy balance that respects everyone's needs and values. Another valuable approach is leading by example. When others witness you respecting your boundaries and handling pushback with grace, it sets a powerful precedent. It encourages them to consider their own boundaries and approach interpersonal challenges with thoughtfulness and empathy. Lastly, don't be disheartened by initial resistance. Change takes time, and consistent reinforcement of your boundaries will gradually shift the dynamics of your relationships in a positive direction. Your commitment to self-respect and healthy boundaries will not only benefit you but also inspire those around you to embrace similar principles. Remember, handling pushback with grace is an art that requires practice and patience. Over time, it will become second nature, and you'll find yourself navigating challenging conversations with confidence and composure.

Boundaries in Work and Play

Now that we've delved into handling pushback, it's time to explore how setting boundaries applies to both our professional and personal lives. When it comes to work, establishing clear boundaries is crucial for maintaining a healthy work-life balance. Too often, we find ourselves glued to our devices, responding to emails round the clock, or taking on more than we can handle out of fear of disappointing others. It's vital to recognize that saying no to overcommitment doesn't equate to laziness; rather, it's an act of self-preservation that ultimately benefits everyone involved. Setting clear expectations with colleagues or clients about response times and availability can reduce stress and prevent burnout. Similarly, in our personal lives, boundaries are essential for protecting our mental and emotional wellbeing. This means learning to say no to social engagements when we're feeling drained, prioritizing self-care without guilt, and recognizing and respecting our limits in relationships. In a world where FOMO (fear of missing out) looms large, it's important to remember that declining invitations or taking time for yourself isn't selfish—it's an act of self-respect. When it comes to enforcing these boundaries, open communication is key. Whether in the workplace or among friends and family, explaining your needs and limits with honesty and empathy can foster understanding and respect. Of course, there may be instances of pushback or resistance, but staying firm while maintaining kindness can help others recognize and appreciate your boundaries. Building a supportive tribe is also a game-changer when it comes to upholding our boundaries. Surrounding ourselves with people who celebrate our self-care efforts and encourage us to prioritize our needs creates a positive environment for growth. Through shared experiences and mutual understanding, our support network can become a source of strength, reinforcing the value of our boundaries and offering encouragement when sticking to them becomes challenging. By striking the right balance between work and play, and by setting and honoring our boundaries in both realms, we pave the way for a more fulfilling, sustainable lifestyle. Remember, establishing boundaries isn't about exclusion or isolation; it's about creating space for authentic connections, meaningful experiences, and personal growth.

Building a Supportive Tribe

Building a supportive tribe is like assembling your dream team, both personally and professionally. These are the people who lift you up when you're feeling low, cheer for you on your biggest wins, and offer a listening ear when life gets tough. Your tribe should consist of individuals who truly understand and respect your boundaries while encouraging you to grow. When it comes to creating this tribe, quality certainly trumps quantity. It's not about having an extensive social circle, but rather having a handful of deeply meaningful connections. Look for individuals who share your values, inspire you to be your best self, and provide constructive support. This might be a mix of friends, mentors, colleagues, and family members. And remember, there's nothing wrong with letting go of toxic relationships that don't serve your wellbeing. Nurturing your tribe involves reciprocity. It's not just about receiving support, but also offering it in return. Be present for your tribe members, celebrate their victories, and lend a helping hand when they need it. The trust and loyalty you build within your tribe will foster a sense of security and belonging that's essential for your overall happiness and success. Communication is key in maintaining these connections. Regular check-ins, honest conversations, and shared experiences help strengthen the bonds within your tribe. In the realm of business, having a supportive network can significantly impact your growth and resilience. Seek out mentors and peers who have been where you want to go and who can offer guidance and insight. Collaborative partnerships and a network of professionals with diverse skills can open doors and provide valuable resources to help you navigate challenges and opportunities. Surrounding yourself with positive, like-minded individuals can also boost your creativity, inspire new ideas, and keep you motivated during tough times. Ultimately, building a supportive tribe is about surrounding yourself with people who elevate you, challenge you, and provide a sense of community. Your tribe becomes your chosen family, the ones who understand your journey and are invested in your success. Cultivating these relationships requires effort, but the rewards of having a tribe that champions your personal and professional growth are immeasurable.

Balancing Compassion and Self-Care

We've all heard the saying, 'You can't pour from an empty cup,' and it couldn't be more true when it comes to balancing compassion and self-care. It's all too easy to lose yourself in the act of caring for others, whether it's your team, your clients, or your loved ones, but neglecting your own well-being can have detrimental effects. Balancing compassion means finding that sweet spot where you can empathize and support others without sacrificing your own mental and emotional health. So, how do you strike this delicate balance? It starts with a healthy dose of self-awareness. Recognize your limits and understand that it's okay to prioritize your own needs. Self-care isn't selfish; it's essential. It might mean setting aside time for activities that recharge your batteries, whether it's yoga, meditation, or simply spending time in nature. Understand what brings you joy and make it a non-negotiable part of your routine. At the same time, it's vital to approach compassion with intention. Practice active listening and empathy without internalizing the pain of others. Offer support without taking on their burdens. Remember, you're a source of strength, not an emotional dumping ground. As you navigate this delicate dance, surrounding yourself with a supportive tribe becomes even more crucial. Lean on like-minded individuals who understand the importance of both compassion and self-care. Seek out mentors and friends who embody this balance and learn from their example. Setting boundaries is also key – know when to step back and recharge, and communicate this need clearly to those around you. Ultimately, finding equilibrium between compassion and self-care is a deeply personal journey. It requires continuous reflection, adjustment, and self-compassion. Embrace the process, knowing that by taking care of yourself, you'll be better equipped to offer genuine, sustainable support to those who rely on you.

Moving Forward: Embracing Your New Balance

Now that you've navigated the delicate dance of balancing compassion and self-care, it's time to forge ahead with a newfound sense of equilibrium. Embracing your new balance is all about integrating the lessons learned into your daily life as you move forward. It means making a conscious effort to prioritize your well-being without feeling guilty, while also maintaining consideration for others around you. As you transition into this phase, take a moment to reflect on the progress you've made towards setting boundaries and saying no when necessary. Remember those instances where you stayed true to yourself and resisted the urge to overcommit. Acknowledge the positive impact these actions have had on your mental and emotional health, and use these victories as fuel to propel you towards sustained harmony. Embracing your new balance requires a proactive mindset. It's about embracing the fact that you're entitled to joy and fulfillment, and that preserving your boundaries plays a vital role in achieving this. Whether it's carving out dedicated 'you' time each day or scheduling activities that recharge your spirit, make a steadfast commitment to honor these efforts. This may involve gracefully declining invitations that do not align with your values or prioritizing solitude when needed. Moreover, part of this transition involves openly communicating your needs to those around you. Whether it's in your personal or professional circles, initiating transparent conversations about your boundaries can foster stronger, more authentic connections. Embracing your new balance means being unapologetically honest about what you require to thrive, and inviting others to reciprocate this openness. It's also vital to remain adaptable as you embrace this newfound equilibrium. Life is dynamic, and there will inevitably be moments that challenge your resolve. When faced with such situations, lean on the support system you've cultivated and be kind to yourself. Recognize that setbacks are part of the journey, and each hurdle surmounted only strengthens your resilience. Lastly, as you continue navigating this transformative phase, celebrate your milestones and milestones of growth. Each instance where you assert your boundaries and honor your well-being is a triumph worth acknowledging. By doing so, you'll reaffirm your dedication to the pursuit of balance and ultimately inspire others to do the same. Remember, this process is ongoing, and as you move forward, carry the wisdom acquired with you as a compass guiding you towards a life enriched by harmony and serenity.

Cultivating Resilience

Understanding What Resilience Really Means

Resilience is more than just bouncing back from tough situations. It's about thriving and growing despite adversity. When life throws curveballs, being resilient means having the inner strength to navigate through challenges without losing hope. It's like a muscle that gets stronger with every hurdle you overcome. Understanding resilience means acknowledging that setbacks are a natural part of life – it's not about avoiding them, but rather how we respond to them that truly matters. Resilience is about finding the courage to weather the storms, adapt to change, and emerge even stronger on the other side. It's the ability to maintain a positive outlook, tap into your support network, and keep moving forward when the going gets tough. By understanding what resilience really means, you can reframe setbacks as opportunities for growth, learn from experiences, and become better equipped to handle whatever comes your way.

Bouncing Back vs. Bouncing Forward

Let's take a closer look at the idea of bouncing back versus bouncing forward. Bouncing back is often seen as returning to the previous state after facing a challenge or adversity. It's like hitting a roadblock, stopping, and then somehow finding a way to get back on track. It's definitely a part of resilience, but it's not the whole picture. Bouncing forward, on the other hand, involves using adversity as a catalyst for growth and positive change. When you bounce forward, you don't just return to your previous state – you come out stronger, wiser, and more capable than before. It's about turning obstacles into opportunities and using them to propel yourself forward. Think of it as not just surviving, but thriving in the face of adversity. This concept of bouncing forward shifts the narrative from simply enduring challenges to actively leveraging them for personal and professional development. It's about harnessing the power of resilience to create a better version of yourself and your circumstances. As we delve deeper into this concept, we'll explore practical strategies and mindset shifts that can help you adopt a bouncing forward mentality in your own life and business endeavors. Get ready to embrace the notion of using setbacks as stepping stones and turning adversities into advantages.

Stress-Busting Strategies for Real Life

We all know that running a business, or just dealing with the everyday demands of life, can be mega stressful. But here's the thing: stress doesn't have to rule your world. There are tons of strategies you can use to bust through that stress and come out on top. First up, let's talk about the magic of exercise. Getting those endorphins pumping is like a natural mood booster – it helps to lift the weight of the world off your shoulders. Whether it's hitting the gym, taking a long walk, or even just dancing around your living room, moving your body can work wonders. Then there's the power of mindfulness. Ever tried meditation? It's not just some mystical hippie stuff – it's a legit way to calm your mind and regain control over your thoughts. And speaking of thoughts, learning to reframe negative thinking can really shift your perspective. Instead of getting bogged down by the 'what ifs' and worst-case scenarios, try focusing on what you can control and finding the silver linings in tough situations. Let's not forget about making time for things that bring you joy. Whether it's indulging in a hobby, spending quality time with loved ones, or laughing until your stomach hurts, injecting fun and relaxation into your schedule is non-negotiable. Oh, and one last thing – don't underestimate the power of a good night's sleep. Catching those Z's isn't just for the lazy; it's essential for recharging your batteries and keeping your stress levels in check. So, next time you feel the pressure mounting, remember these stress-busting strategies and give yourself the care and attention you deserve. You've got this!

The Power of a Positive Perspective

Having a positive perspective can completely shift how we approach challenges and setbacks. It's not about ignoring the difficulties or pretending everything is always perfect, but rather about finding a silver lining and cultivating an optimistic mindset. When we're able to see the good even in tough situations, it fuels our resilience and gives us the strength to keep moving forward. Think about it: when faced with a problem, focusing on what's going wrong tends to make us feel overwhelmed and disheartened. However, shifting our focus to what we can learn from the situation or how it might lead to new opportunities can truly empower us. Cultivating this type of mindset takes practice, but it's a game-changer. Instead of letting negativity take over, intentionally look for the positive aspects within any challenge. This doesn't mean being overly cheerful all the time; it's about understanding that setbacks are temporary and that we have the ability to overcome them. Additionally, the way we talk to ourselves internally greatly influences our perspective. Choosing to use encouraging and affirming self-talk can significantly boost our resilience. When we catch ourselves slipping into negative self-talk, consciously reframe those thoughts into something more constructive. Remember, small shifts in perspective can yield big results. Encouraging others around you to maintain a positive outlook also helps bolster your own resilience. When everyone is focused on finding solutions and staying positive, it creates a supportive environment where individuals can thrive. As you encounter challenges on your journey, remember that maintaining a positive perspective is like having a secret weapon in your arsenal. It keeps you grounded and motivated, allowing you to tackle whatever comes your way with grace and determination.

Building Your Support Squad

In the game of entrepreneurship, having a strong support network can be your secret weapon. Your support squad includes the people who have your back and lift you up when times get tough. It's not just about having friends who cheer you on, but also about surrounding yourself with mentors, advisors, and like-minded individuals who understand the entrepreneurial journey. These are the people you can turn to for advice, guidance, or simply a listening ear. First and foremost, your support squad should include fellow entrepreneurs or business owners who can relate to your experiences. Connecting with others who share similar challenges and triumphs can provide a sense of camaraderie and validation. They can offer insights, share resources, and even become valuable collaborators as you navigate the ups and downs of running a business. Mentors and advisors are also indispensable members of your support squad. Seek out individuals who have walked the path you're on and have valuable wisdom to impart. Their guidance can help you avoid common pitfalls, make informed decisions, and gain clarity during uncertain times. Whether it's a formal mentorship relationship or casual networking, surrounding yourself with seasoned professionals can be a game-changer. Don't underestimate the power of family and friends as part of your support squad. While they may not fully grasp the intricacies of entrepreneurship, their unwavering belief in you can be a powerful source of motivation and encouragement. Lean on them for moral support, celebrate your wins together, and draw strength from the love and positivity they bring into your life. Additionally, consider joining entrepreneurial communities or networks, both locally and online. These platforms can provide access to valuable resources, diverse perspectives, and opportunities for collaboration. Whether it's a co-working space, industry-specific groups, or online forums, being part of a community can combat the isolation that often accompanies the entrepreneurial journey. Remember, building your support squad is not just about seeking help; it's also about offering support in return. Be willing to listen, contribute, and pay it forward within your network. By nurturing these relationships and actively participating in your support squad, you can create a robust safety net that bolsters your resilience and propels you towards success.

Embracing Failure as a Friend

Failure is often seen as the biggest fear and something we should avoid at all costs. However, what if we shift our perspective and start looking at failure as a significant part of success? Embracing failure as a friend doesn't mean seeking out failure or refusing to learn from mistakes, but rather acknowledging that setbacks and missteps are an integral part of growth and forward progress. It's essential to reframe the way we view failure. Instead of seeing it as a dead end, think of it as a detour on the road to success. Each failure holds within it valuable lessons and opportunities for growth. By embracing failure, we can release the fear of making mistakes and feel liberated to take risks and try new things. One way to embrace failure is by adopting a growth mindset. Rather than seeing your abilities and talents as fixed traits, understand that they can be developed through dedication and hard work. When you encounter failure, don't dwell on the negative aspects; instead, focus on what you can learn from the experience and how you can improve for the future. Embracing failure as a friend also requires self-compassion. It's okay to feel disappointed when things don't go as planned, but it's important to treat yourself with kindness and understanding. Remember that everyone experiences failure at some point, and it's a natural part of life and progress. Moreover, failure allows us to test our resilience and adaptability. It strengthens our ability to bounce back, enhances our problem-solving skills, and fosters creativity. When we see failure as a friend, it becomes a source of motivation and drive, pushing us to strive for better solutions and outcomes. In the entrepreneurial world, failure is almost inevitable. Many successful entrepreneurs attribute their achievements to the valuable lessons learned from previous failures. They understand that each setback brings them closer to success and view failure not as an endpoint, but as a stepping stone to greatness. Ultimately, by embracing failure as a friend, we open ourselves up to endless possibilities and pave the way for personal and professional development. It reshapes our mindset, fuels our resilience, and propels us toward success with a newfound sense of purpose and determination.

Finding Calm in the Chaos

Life can be chaotic and overwhelming at times, with deadlines to meet, unexpected challenges to overcome, and personal responsibilities to juggle. In the midst of this whirlwind, finding moments of calm is essential for maintaining resilience and overall well-being. One effective strategy for finding calm in chaos is to practice mindfulness. Whether through meditation, deep breathing exercises, or simply taking a few minutes to focus on the present moment, mindfulness can help ground you and provide a sense of peace amidst the storm. Another approach is to create physical spaces that promote calmness. Consider adding a cozy corner in your workspace, where you can retreat when feeling overwhelmed. This designated space can serve as a refuge, allowing you to decompress and reset. Additionally, establishing daily routines can bring a sense of order and stability to your life, offering a respite from the chaos. Incorporating regular exercise, adequate rest, and healthy eating habits into your routine can also significantly contribute to your ability to navigate tumultuous times. Moreover, seeking solace in nature can offer a powerful antidote to chaos. Spending time outdoors, whether it's a walk in the park or simply sitting in a tranquil garden, can provide a much-needed break from the demands of daily life. Finally, fostering meaningful connections with others can act as an anchor in turbulent times. Lean on friends, family, or even colleagues for support and companionship. A listening ear or a friendly conversation can provide comfort and perspective when everything else seems overwhelming. By actively seeking out strategies to find calm within chaos, you can bolster your resilience and equip yourself to face life's challenges with greater ease and composure.

Resilience in Health and Wellness

When it comes to resilience, we often talk about mental and emotional strength, but we can't overlook the significance of physical health and wellness. Our bodies and minds are deeply interconnected, and taking care of our physical well-being is crucial for building resilience. With good health as a foundation, we're better equipped to weather life's storms and come out stronger on the other side. First and foremost, let's address the importance of sleep. Quality rest is non-negotiable when it comes to resilience. It's during sleep that our bodies repair and recharge, setting the stage for us to face challenges with clarity and energy. Creating a consistent sleep routine and prioritizing restful slumber can make a world of difference in how we handle adversity. Nutrition also plays a pivotal role in resilience. A balanced diet rich in fruits, vegetables, lean proteins, and healthy fats provides the essential nutrients our bodies need to function at their best. Fueling our bodies with proper nutrition not only bolsters physical resilience but also impacts our mental well-being, contributing to a more balanced and stable state of mind. Moreover, regular exercise is a powerful tool in cultivating resilience. Physical activity not only enhances our physical strength and endurance but also releases endorphins, the body's natural stress-relievers, promoting a positive mindset and reducing anxiety. Whether it's a brisk walk, yoga, or hitting the gym, finding an exercise routine that suits your preferences and lifestyle is imperative for maintaining resilience. In addition to these lifestyle factors, it's essential to prioritize regular check-ups and preventative healthcare. Staying on top of your physical health through regular medical appointments and screenings allows you to address any potential issues proactively, preventing them from becoming larger obstacles in the future. Taking a proactive approach to your health empowers you to face challenges head-on, knowing that you're in the best possible shape to do so. Lastly, but certainly not least, don't underestimate the power of relaxation and self-care. Setting aside time for activities that bring you joy and peace, whether it's reading, spending time in nature, or practicing mindfulness, contributes to overall resilience. It's not just about pushing through, but also about finding moments to recharge and rejuvenate, fostering a strong and resilient foundation for all aspects of life.

Mindset Makeover: Adapt and Overcome

Let's face it – life throws curveballs when we least expect them. How we react to these challenges can make all the difference in our personal and professional lives. Enter the mindset makeover: a powerful tool for adapting and overcoming adversity with grace and resilience. It's all about rewiring your thought patterns to embrace change, learn from setbacks, and emerge stronger than ever. First off, let's ditch the idea of a fixed mindset – the belief that our abilities and intelligence are set in stone. Instead, cultivate a growth mindset, recognizing that we can develop and improve through dedication and hard work. This shift in perspective opens up a world of possibilities and encourages us to view obstacles as opportunities for growth. Next, it's time to reframe failure. Rather than seeing it as a roadblock, view it as a stepping stone on the path to success. Embracing failure as a natural part of the journey allows us to take risks, learn from mistakes, and pivot when necessary. Remember, every setback is a lesson in disguise. As you navigate the daily grind, practice mindfulness to stay present and centered. Take a few moments each day to breathe, reflect, and reset. This simple act can bring clarity and calm, offering a fresh perspective on any challenges that come your way. Moreover, surround yourself with a support network of positive, like-minded individuals who uplift and inspire you. Share your experiences, seek advice, and offer encouragement in return. Building this circle of trust can provide the emotional boost needed to tackle tough times with unwavering resolve. Finally, remember that adapting and overcoming isn't just about powering through – it's also about knowing when to recharge. Prioritize self-care, nurture your well-being, and give yourself permission to take breaks. Rest and rejuvenation are integral to maintaining a resilient mindset in the face of adversity. So, let's kickstart our mindset makeover and pave the way for triumph in the midst of trials. With a growth mindset, an embrace of failure, mindfulness practices, a supportive tribe, and self-care rituals, you'll be primed to adapt and overcome anything life throws your way.

Putting It All Together in Your Daily Grind

So, you've made it through the muck and have come out on the other side, victorious. But now what? How do you take all the wisdom and tools you've accumulated and apply them to your daily hustle – the endless cycle of tasks, challenges, and opportunities that make up your grind? Well, let's break it down. First things first, start your day with intention. Set aside time for reflection, goal-setting, and visualizing success. This simple practice can help center your mind and give you a clear focus to carry into your day. Once you're in the thick of it, leverage your newfound stress-busting strategies. Whether it's taking a power walk during lunch, practicing deep breathing in between meetings, or scheduling regular breaks to step away from your desk, find ways to infuse pockets of calm into your bustling schedule. Remember, resilience isn't just about reacting to hardships – it's also about proactively fortifying yourself against potential stressors. Keep your support squad close. Reach out to your network for advice, brainstorming sessions, or simply a listening ear. Building a sense of community and shared experience can help alleviate the weight of challenges and keep you grounded. Embrace failure as a friend, not a foe. See setbacks as opportunities to learn and grow, and keep moving forward. Cultivate a gratitude practice. Take a moment each day to acknowledge the wins, however small they may seem. This positive perspective can fuel your resilience and bolster your mental fortitude. Make conscious choices when it comes to health and wellness. Eat nourishing foods, move your body, and prioritize sleep. A healthy foundation is essential for weathering the storms of entrepreneurship. And perhaps most importantly, check your mindset. Stay flexible, open-minded, and adaptable. As your business evolves, so too should your approach. Be willing to pivot, innovate, and explore new avenues. The ability to adapt is a cornerstone of resilience. So, there you have it – a blueprint for integrating resilience into your day-to-day grind. With these strategies in your arsenal, you'll be better equipped to navigate the inevitable twists and turns of entrepreneurial life.

The Long Game: Building a Business for the Future

Vision: Your North Star

Setting a clear and compelling vision is crucial for steering your business toward future success. Your vision is like a North Star, providing direction, guidance, and inspiration for you and your team. It's the big picture that captures the essence of what you want to achieve and the impact you aim to create. When crafting your vision, consider what sets your business apart, the value it brings to customers and society, and the legacy you want to leave behind. This is not just about profits; it's about purpose. A strong vision can ignite passion and drive within your team, aligning everyone toward a common goal. It becomes the foundation for decision-making, strategy development, and resource allocation. With a compelling vision, you can rally your employees, attract investors, and earn customer loyalty. It also serves as a compass during times of uncertainty and change, guiding your business through challenges and opportunities. Your vision should be bold yet achievable, inspiring people to join you on the journey while providing a roadmap for growth and expansion. Remember, a powerful vision is a magnet for talent, a catalyst for innovation, and a source of resilience when facing adversity. As you articulate your vision, communicate it authentically and consistently across your organization, ensuring that everyone understands and aligns with the overarching purpose. Revisit and refine your vision periodically, especially as your business evolves. The clarity and strength of your vision will determine the enduring impact and relevance of your business in the years to come. Embrace the process of crafting your North Star, for it will illuminate the path to a future filled with purpose and possibility.

Embracing Change and Innovation

Change is a constant in the world of business, and those who adapt and innovate are the ones who thrive. Embracing change means being open to new ideas, methods, and technologies. It's about recognizing that the business landscape is always evolving and being willing to pivot when necessary. Innovation goes hand in hand with change. It's about finding creative solutions to challenges and constantly looking for ways to improve and grow. Whether it's streamlining processes, developing new products, or entering untapped markets, innovation keeps your business relevant and competitive. To truly embrace change and innovation, you need to foster a culture that values creativity, experimentation, and calculated risk-taking. Encouraging your team to think outside the box and rewarding initiative can lead to breakthrough ideas and fresh approaches. Another key aspect of embracing change and innovation is staying informed about industry trends and emerging technologies. Being proactive about learning and adapting to new developments can give your business a strategic edge and help you anticipate and prepare for shifts in the market. It's also important to remember that embracing change doesn't mean constantly chasing after every new trend. It's about discerning which changes are worth pursuing and align with your long-term vision. Sometimes, the most innovative move is staying true to your core values while finding new ways to express them. In summary, embracing change and innovation is about remaining agile, curious, and forward-thinking. By doing so, you're positioning your business not just to survive, but to thrive in an ever-evolving landscape.

Investing in People

Investing in people is the cornerstone of building a successful and sustainable business for the future. It's not just about hiring employees; it's about nurturing a culture of growth, empowerment, and support. When you invest in your team, you're investing in the heart and soul of your business. One of the key aspects of investing in people is providing opportunities for professional development and growth. This can include ongoing training, mentorship programs, and leadership development initiatives. By empowering your employees to expand their skills and knowledge, you're not only enhancing their individual potential but also contributing to the overall strength of your organization. Additionally, fostering a positive work environment that prioritizes employee well-being and work-life balance is imperative. When employees feel valued and supported, they are more likely to be engaged, productive, and committed to the success of the business. Moreover, transparent and open communication channels play a crucial role in creating a sense of belonging and trust within the team. As a leader, it's essential to listen to your employees, understand their concerns, and involve them in decision-making processes. Recognizing and appreciating the efforts of your team members through rewards, recognition programs, and a culture of appreciation goes a long way in reinforcing their contributions to the company. Remember, investing in people goes beyond the confines of the workplace. Supporting diversity, inclusivity, and equality within your organization fosters an environment where everyone feels respected and valued. This not only leads to a more innovative and creative team but also strengthens your company's reputation in the market. Ultimately, investing in people is an ongoing commitment; it's about cultivating a community of individuals who are motivated, inspired, and dedicated to the shared goals and vision of the business.

Sustainable Foundations

In the fast-paced world of business, it's easy to get caught up in the immediate demands and challenges. However, building a business for the long haul requires a solid and sustainable foundation. This foundation encompasses multiple aspects that are vital for the longevity and success of your enterprise. At its core, sustainable foundations involve creating structures and processes that can withstand the test of time. This means establishing environmentally friendly practices, ethical operations, and a commitment to corporate social responsibility. As businesses worldwide face increasing scrutiny regarding their impact on the planet and society, having sustainable foundations is not just a nice-to-have, but a necessity for survival and growth. Moreover, financial stability plays a crucial role in sustaining a business. This involves prudent financial management, including managing cash flow, reducing debt, and making strategic investments. A healthy balance sheet provides a safety net during economic downturns and allows for strategic expansion when opportunities arise. Furthermore, cultivating a positive company culture is integral to sustainable foundations. Fostering an environment where employees feel valued, respected, and motivated leads to higher retention rates, increased productivity, and a stronger reputation in the market. Investing in professional development, offering work-life balance, and promoting diversity and inclusion are essential elements of this cultural fabric. Additionally, diversifying revenue streams and avoiding over-reliance on a single product or service mitigates risk and ensures resilience in the face of changing market dynamics. This could involve expanding into new markets, developing complementary offerings, or embracing innovative business models to future-proof your revenue generation. Lastly, embracing digital transformation is an indispensable component of sustainable foundations. Leveraging technology not only increases operational efficiency but also opens new avenues for reaching customers, analyzing data, and staying ahead of industry trends. Whether through automation, streamlined communication channels, or adopting cutting-edge tools, integrating technology into the fabric of your business is paramount. By establishing these sustainable foundations, you position your business to weather storms, adapt to evolving landscapes, and thrive in the long run. Remember, building for the future requires laying sturdy groundwork today.

Adapting to Market Shifts

In today's fast-paced business landscape, adapting to market shifts is crucial for the long-term success of any venture. Market shifts can be triggered by technological advancements, changes in consumer behavior, or unexpected global events. It's essential for entrepreneurs and business leaders to remain agile and responsive to these shifts to stay ahead of the curve. One way to adapt to market shifts is by staying informed about industry trends and understanding the evolving needs and preferences of your target audience. This could involve conducting regular market research, gathering customer feedback, and closely monitoring competitors. By staying attuned to market dynamics, you can identify emerging opportunities and potential threats early on. Flexibility is another key element in adapting to market shifts. Being open to adjusting your business strategies, product offerings, or operational processes based on changing market conditions can help you stay relevant and competitive. Embracing new technologies and innovative practices can also give your business an edge in responding to market shifts. Whether it's integrating e-commerce solutions, adopting data analytics tools, or implementing efficient supply chain management systems, leveraging technology can enhance your ability to adapt swiftly to evolving market demands. Moreover, fostering a culture of creativity and resilience within your team can empower them to proactively address market shifts. Encouraging open dialogue, experimentation, and calculated risk-taking can inspire fresh ideas and novel approaches to navigate market changes. Lastly, building robust relationships with suppliers, distributors, and industry partners can provide added support in responding to market shifts. Collaborative partnerships can offer valuable insights, resources, and mutually beneficial opportunities to collectively navigate market challenges and capitalize on emerging trends. Adapting to market shifts requires a proactive and dynamic approach that recognizes the inevitability of change in the business environment. By cultivating a responsive and forward-thinking mindset, businesses can not only weather market shifts but also find new avenues for growth and innovation.

Balancing Risk and Reward

In the ever-changing landscape of business, finding the balance between risk and reward is crucial for long-term success. Taking risks can be exhilarating and offer the potential for significant growth, but it's essential to weigh these decisions with a clear understanding of the potential rewards and possible consequences. One key aspect of balancing risk and reward is conducting thorough risk assessments. Identifying potential risks allows you to develop strategies to mitigate them, reducing the potential negative impact on your business. By critically evaluating the potential outcomes of your decisions, you can effectively weigh the risks against the potential rewards. Furthermore, embracing calculated risks often requires a willingness to innovate and adapt. These risks may involve venturing into new markets, investing in groundbreaking technologies, or implementing disruptive business models. While these endeavors carry inherent risks, they also present opportunities for substantial growth and competitive advantage. Effective risk management involves being agile and responsive to market shifts and customer needs. By staying attuned to industry trends and consumer behavior, you can make informed decisions about when and where to take calculated risks. This adaptability allows you to navigate uncertainty while positioning your business to capitalize on emerging opportunities. However, it's important to recognize that not all risks are worth taking. Understanding the difference between strategic risks that align with your long-term vision and reckless gambles is vital. It's about striking a balance that aligns with your goals, resources, and the overall well-being of your business. Additionally, creating a culture that encourages calculated risk-taking while prioritizing learning from both successes and failures is instrumental in fostering a proactive approach to risk management. Embracing a mindset that views setbacks as learning experiences can transform perceived failures into valuable lessons that propel your business forward. Ultimately, the ability to balance risk and reward is a skill honed through experience and a deep understanding of your industry.

By carefully weighing the potential gains and losses, adapting to changing circumstances, and fostering a mindset of calculated innovation, you can navigate the complexities of risk management while maximizing the potential for sustainable growth and success.

Leveraging Technology for Growth

In today's fast-paced business landscape, technology plays a pivotal role in driving growth and staying ahead of the competition. Leveraging technology for growth means embracing digital tools and platforms to streamline operations, enhance productivity, and reach wider audiences. One of the fundamental aspects of leveraging technology involves investing in scalable and adaptable systems that can evolve with your business. From cloud-based software solutions to automation tools, modern technology offers a myriad of opportunities to optimize processes and drive efficiency. By harnessing these tools, businesses can allocate resources effectively, freeing up time and capital for strategic initiatives. Moreover, technology also enables seamless communication and collaboration among team members, regardless of geographical barriers. This fosters innovation and creativity, allowing for diverse perspectives to contribute to problem-solving and decision-making. Another crucial aspect of technology-driven growth is data analytics. Through advanced analytics tools, businesses can gain valuable insights into consumer behavior, market trends, and operational performance. This data-driven approach empowers informed decision-making, helping businesses tailor their strategies for maximum impact. Furthermore, technology facilitates personalized customer experiences through CRM systems, social media engagement, and targeted marketing campaigns. Enhanced customer interactions not only foster loyalty but also drive positive word-of-mouth referrals, expanding the business's reach. Embracing emerging technologies such as AI, machine learning, and IoT presents exciting avenues for innovation and product development. These cutting-edge technologies have the potential to revolutionize products and services, offering unique value propositions to customers. Lastly, cybersecurity and risk management are integral considerations when leveraging technology for growth. Protecting sensitive data, ensuring privacy compliance, and mitigating cyber threats are paramount in safeguarding business continuity and reputation. By proactively addressing these concerns, businesses can build trust with customers and stakeholders while minimizing potential disruptions. Ultimately, leveraging technology for growth requires a strategic, forward-thinking approach that embraces innovation, efficiency, and a customer-centric mindset.

Nurturing Customer Relationships

Nurturing customer relationships is like tending to a garden – it requires dedication, care, and attention to flourish. In the digital age, where competition is fierce and choices are abundant, fostering strong connections with your customers is essential for long-term success. It's not just about making a sale; it's about creating meaningful interactions that build loyalty and advocacy. So, how do you nurture these relationships effectively? Firstly, it's crucial to understand your customers on a deeper level. What are their pain points, desires, and preferences? Utilize customer data and feedback to personalize their experiences and tailor your offerings to meet their individual needs. Show genuine appreciation by acknowledging their loyalty, whether through personalized thank-you notes, exclusive offers, or recognizing milestones in your business relationship. Engage with them beyond transactions – share valuable content, seek their input, and invite them to be part of your brand's story. Remember, communication is key. Be responsive, empathetic, and proactive in addressing any concerns or questions. Strive to exceed their expectations at every touchpoint, from initial contact to post-purchase support. Furthermore, transparency and authenticity are non-negotiable. Customers appreciate honesty and integrity; admit mistakes when they occur and take responsibility to make things right. By doing so, you'll earn their trust and respect.

Additionally, consider creating a community around your brand where customers can connect with each other and with you. Encourage user-generated content, hold events, and foster a sense of belonging. Lastly, consistently evaluate and improve your customer relationship strategies. Keep abreast of industry trends, gather insights, and evolve with your customers' evolving needs. Remember, happy customers are your best advocates and can fuel sustainable growth. By nurturing strong, lasting relationships, you'll not only gain loyal patrons but also ambassadors who will champion your brand far and wide.

Building a Brand that Lasts

When it comes to building a brand that stands the test of time, it's all about cultivating a unique identity and fostering a deep connection with your audience. A lasting brand isn't just about flashy logos or catchy slogans; it's about building a reputation and relationship that endures. So, how do you go about achieving this? Firstly, authenticity is key. Your brand should reflect your values and resonate with your target demographic on a genuine level. This means being transparent, honest, and consistent in your messaging and actions. People are drawn to brands they can trust and relate to. Next, consistency across all touchpoints is vital. Whether it's your website, social media, packaging, or customer service, every interaction should embody your brand's essence and voice. This creates a cohesive and memorable experience for your audience. Moreover, focusing on quality, not just in your products or services but also in every aspect of your brand's representation, reinforces the idea of reliability. Additionally, storytelling has the power to humanize your brand. Sharing the journey, values, and impact of your business creates an emotional bond with your audience. Furthermore, community engagement and social responsibility play significant roles. Supporting causes, engaging in meaningful conversations, and actively listening to feedback demonstrate that your brand cares about more than just profit. Lastly, adaptable branding that can evolve and stay relevant over time is crucial. The ability to embrace change while staying true to your core values allows your brand to remain both timeless and contemporary. Building a brand that lasts involves an ongoing commitment to these principles, and it's this dedication that paves the way for enduring success.

Thinking Generationally

When it comes to building a business for the future, one crucial aspect is the ability to think generationally. This means looking beyond short-term gains and considering how your decisions today will impact not only the next few years but also the legacy you leave for future generations. Thinking generationally requires a shift in mindset – it's about prioritizing sustainability, longevity, and impact over quick wins. To achieve this, it's essential to focus on creating a culture of stewardship within your organization. This involves instilling values that emphasize the responsibility of current leaders to preserve and enhance the business for those who will follow. One way to start thinking generationally is by establishing a clear succession plan. Identifying and developing talent within your company ensures that there are capable leaders prepared to carry the torch in the years to come. Moreover, it fosters an environment where employees feel valued and invested in the organization's future. Beyond internal talent, consider how your business can contribute positively to the communities it operates in. This may involve sustainable practices, community engagement initiatives, or philanthropic endeavors that leave a lasting, positive impact. Furthermore, technology plays a pivotal role in shaping the future of any business. By leveraging innovative tools and staying abreast of industry advancements, you can position your company as forward-thinking and adaptable. Embracing renewable energy sources, implementing eco-friendly processes, and reducing waste not only benefit the environment but also contribute to a more sustainable business model. When thinking generationally, it's important to consider the broader societal and environmental implications of your business operations. Are there ways your company can minimize its carbon footprint? Can you foster diversity and inclusion both within the workplace and through your products and services? These considerations have far-reaching effects and can help establish a positive legacy for your business. In summary, thinking generationally is about setting the stage for a thriving, impactful business that transcends immediate profitability. It involves purposefully laying the groundwork for a sustainable, responsible, and enduring enterprise that contributes positively to the world at large. By embracing this mindset, you're not just building a business for the present – you're crafting a legacy that will be cherished for generations to come.

Conclusion: Living a Life of Purpose and Abundance

Reflecting on the Journey

As we look back on the journey we've taken together, it's only natural to feel a whirlwind of emotions. From the early days of skepticism and uncertainty to the moments of clarity and inspiration, each step has contributed to our growth and understanding. Remember the challenges that seemed insurmountable at first? They transformed into opportunities for learning and adaptation. Those late nights of doubt and worry eventually led to breakthroughs and a newfound sense of resilience. We navigated through uncharted territories, embraced change, and celebrated victories both big and small. It's incredible how every setback, every detour, and every victory played a role in shaping our path to purpose. Reflecting on this journey allows us to appreciate the full spectrum of experiences – the exhilarating highs and the humbling lows that have enriched our lives in ways we never could have imagined. Each chapter of this adventure has painted a unique picture of growth, perseverance, and the pursuit of something greater than ourselves. And while the destination may still be on the horizon, the insights gained and the connections made along the way have already made this journey an invaluable part of our lives. The beauty of reflection lies in its power to illuminate our progress, offering a tapestry of memories and lessons that serve as the foundation for our continued pursuit of purpose. So, let's take a moment to honor the twists and turns, the moments of uncertainty, and the flashes of brilliance that have woven together to create this remarkable journey. Whether you're standing at the summit or embracing a fresh start, remember that the sum of your experiences paints a unique and beautiful picture. As we reflect on the journey, let's carry forward the wisdom gained, the relationships cherished, and the unwavering belief that purpose is not just a destination but a way of life.

Key Takeaways from the Adventure

As we near the end of this incredible journey, it's time to pause and reflect on the invaluable lessons we've learned along the way. One of the most profound takeaways from this adventure is the importance of resilience. We've faced unexpected challenges, yet we've persevered and grown stronger with each hurdle. Remember those moments when you thought you couldn't go on, but you did? That resilience is a superpower that will carry you through any future storms. Another key takeaway is the power of community. Whether it's your team, friends, or family, the support of others has been instrumental in overcoming obstacles and celebrating victories. It's in these connections that we find comfort, inspiration, and the shared joy of success. Never underestimate the impact of surrounding yourself with uplifting and driven individuals. Let's not forget about adaptability. Change is inevitable, and our ability to pivot and embrace new opportunities has been a game-changer. Flexibility has allowed us to navigate uncharted territories and discover hidden potential within ourselves. By embracing change, we've unlocked doors we didn't even know existed. The journey has also reinforced the significance of staying true to our purpose. When we align our actions with our core values, we ignite a passion that fuels our every move. This unwavering commitment to our 'why' has been the guiding force behind every decision and every step forward. And finally, the most precious of all takeaways is the realization that abundance encompasses far more than material wealth. True abundance lies in experiences, relationships, personal growth, and moments of pure joy. It's about savoring life's simple pleasures and finding fulfillment in both professional and personal pursuits. So, as we prepare to embark on new adventures, let's carry these takeaways close to heart. They are the compass that will guide us through the ever-changing landscapes of entrepreneurship and life. With resilience, community, adaptability, purpose, and a holistic view of abundance, we're equipped to conquer whatever comes our way.

The Magic of Embracing Change

Change can be a tricky thing, right? We get so comfortable in our routines that even the thought of something shifting can send shivers down our spine. But let me tell you, my friend, there's real magic in embracing change. Think about it: every time something new comes your way, it's an opportunity for growth and expansion. It's like nature's way of nudging us to level up. Sure, change can be daunting, but it's also where the juiciest experiences are born. When we open our arms and welcome change with a smile, we give ourselves the chance to unearth new passions, learn different skills, and meet fascinating people. And that's just the beginning! Embracing change also sparks creativity and innovation. When we're faced with something unfamiliar, our brains kick into high gear, firing off new ideas and possibilities. Suddenly, we find ourselves thinking outside the box, exploring uncharted territories, and discovering solutions we never knew existed. It's pretty exhilarating, isn't it? Let's not forget the personal growth that comes with change. Each time we adapt to a new situation, we become more resilient, more adaptable, more capable. We start to trust in our ability to handle whatever life throws our way. And that, my friend, is true empowerment. So, the next time change knocks on your door, don't be afraid to invite it in for a cup of tea. Embrace it wholeheartedly, knowing that within its unpredictable dance lies the seeds of transformation and the promise of a richer, more fulfilling life.

Finding Balance: Work, Play, and Everything in Between

Life is a juggling act, isn't it? We're constantly trying to keep all the balls in the air - work, family, friends, hobbies, self-care...the list goes on. It's no wonder we feel frazzled sometimes. But here's the thing – finding balance isn't about allocating equal time to every aspect of your life. It's about prioritizing and being fully present in each moment, whether you're hustling at work or enjoying downtime with loved ones.

Work can be all-consuming, especially when you're passionate about what you do. However, it's crucial to carve out space for play and relaxation. Take a break! Step away from your desk and go for a walk, catch up with a friend, or indulge in a hobby. When you return, you'll be amazed at how much more focused and productive you are. On the flip side, don't let the guilt of not working overshadow your personal life. Embrace the joy of spending time with family or pursuing activities that make your heart sing. All work and no play doesn't just make Jack a dull boy – it makes for a pretty uninspired and burnt-out entrepreneur, too. Recognize that achieving balance is an ongoing process and allow yourself the flexibility to adapt as needed. Remember, it's okay to not have it all figured out. Finding the sweet spot between your professional and personal life is a journey, not a destination. So, be kind to yourself along the way. Allow your schedule to ebb and flow, and don't beat yourself up when things don't go according to plan. Strive for progress, not perfection. Trust me, the universe has a funny way of aligning things when you give yourself permission to breathe. Here's to finding balance, one beautifully imperfect day at a time.

Staying True to Your Why

Do you ever find yourself caught up in the hustle and bustle, feeling like you're on a never-ending treadmill of tasks and responsibilities? It happens to the best of us. In these moments, it's crucial to reconnect with your 'why.' What drives you? What is your ultimate purpose and passion? Staying true to your why means continually reminding yourself of what truly matters to you. It's about aligning your daily actions with your core values and long-term aspirations. When you stay connected to your why, it becomes your anchor, your guiding light in both professional and personal pursuits. Whether it's building a business, nurturing relationships, or seeking personal growth, knowing your why keeps you grounded and focused. It empowers you to make decisions that resonate with your authentic self, rather than simply following the crowd. By staying true to your why, you create a life that is not only driven by success but also enriched with fulfillment and meaning. It's about living intentionally and creating a legacy that extends beyond material achievements. Embracing your why allows you to lead a purpose-driven life, where every action contributes to a greater narrative. Remember, your why may evolve over time, and that's perfectly natural. It's a reflection of your growth and experiences. Embrace this evolution, refine your purpose, and let it inspire you to reach new heights. So, take a moment to reflect on your why. What motivates you? What impact do you want to have on the world? By staying true to your why, you'll find the resilience to navigate challenges, the wisdom to prioritize what truly matters, and the courage to pursue your dreams with unwavering conviction.

Abundance: More Than Just a Bank Balance

When we hear the word 'abundance,' our minds often jump straight to financial wealth, but the concept goes far beyond the digits in our bank accounts. Abundance encompasses a holistic richness in life, embracing an attitude of gratitude towards the diverse blessings that surround us. It's about recognizing and appreciating the abundance of love, joy, health, and meaningful relationships that add depth and color to our existence. It's finding immense wealth in the intangible treasures that money can't buy. To live abundantly is to foster a mindset of plenty, recognizing the abundance of opportunities, experiences, and resources at our disposal. It's about acknowledging the beauty in everyday moments, the richness in human connections, and the abundance of possibilities for personal growth and fulfillment. Cultivating abundance involves shifting our focus from scarcity and lack towards an appreciation for the seemingly small yet profound things that shape our lives. It's about celebrating the abundance of creativity, passion, and purpose that ignites our souls and fuels our endeavors. Embracing abundance isn't just an outlook; it's a way of life – one where we choose to see the glass as not just half full, but brimming over with potential and possibility. When we approach life with an abundance mindset, we open ourselves up to manifold opportunities, experiences, and connections that enrich our journey. It encourages us to view setbacks as temporary roadblocks, knowing that there's an abundance of resilience and strength within us to navigate through challenges. The pursuit of abundance isn't about accumulating possessions, but about experiencing the richness of life in all its forms. It's about being present in the moment, reveling in the abundance of simple pleasures, and cherishing the people who bring warmth and light into our lives. Ultimately, living in abundance means realizing that our capacity for joy, love, and fulfillment is boundless, extending far beyond the confines of material wealth. As we embrace this holistic view of abundance, we open ourselves to a life filled with purpose, connection, and immeasurable riches that money can never buy.

People & Passions: Building Lasting Connections

In the colorful tapestry of life, one of the most vibrant threads is woven by the people we meet and the passions we share. Building lasting connections goes beyond just having a robust network or a full social calendar; it's about nurturing meaningful relationships that uplift and inspire us. Think about the individuals who have made a profound impact on your journey – friends, mentors, colleagues, or even strangers whose words touched your soul. These connections often stem from shared passions, as there's an unspoken magic in being around people who light up when they talk about the things they love. Whether it's discussing a favorite book, geeking out over a mutual hobby, or collaborating on a project, these shared interests breed authentic connections. When you're genuinely invested in someone else's passion, it's like adding another layer to your own life story. The beauty of building lasting connections lies in its reciprocity. It's not just about what others can offer us, but also about how we can contribute to their journey. It's about being a sounding board for their ideas, celebrating their victories, and providing support during the challenging times. These connections become a source of encouragement, motivation, and a reality check when needed. They say that you are the average of the five people you spend the most time with, and there's truth to that. Surrounding yourself with individuals who exude positivity, empathy, determination, and kindness can significantly influence your own mindset and aspirations. However, it's equally important to reciprocate these qualities and be the kind of person you'd want to have in your circle. As we navigate through different stages of life, some connections naturally evolve and stand the test of time. These are the friendships that weather storms, celebrate milestones, and grow alongside us. They become our chosen family, sharing not just our joys, but also our vulnerabilities and fears. While technology has made connecting with others more accessible, the essence of building lasting connections lies in those genuine, heart-to-heart conversations, shared experiences, and creating memories together. It's about the warmth of a hug, the laughter that fills the room, and the unspoken understanding that transcends words. So next time you find yourself in the company of kindred spirits, take a moment to appreciate the art of building these lasting connections – for they not only enrich our lives but also infuse them with purpose, belonging, and a deep sense of fulfillment.

Choosing Joy Every Day

You know those moments when you catch yourself smiling for no reason? That's the joy we're talking about. It could be that first sip of coffee in the morning, a heartfelt chat with a friend, or simply basking in the warmth of the sun. Choosing joy every day isn't about seeking grand gestures or waiting for life-changing events. It's about finding pockets of happiness in the everyday hustle. Maybe it's tuning in to your favorite playlist during a work break, indulging in a guilty pleasure TV show, or savoring a delicious meal. These little sparks of joy add up, guiding you through the challenges and triumphs alike. When you actively seek out these moments, you start to notice them everywhere – in the laughter of loved ones, the beauty of nature, or the satisfaction of a job well done. Sometimes, choosing joy means letting go of what no longer serves you, whether it's a toxic relationship, a draining commitment, or self-doubt. By making room for positivity and gratitude, you pave the way for more joy to flow into your life. It's not always easy, of course. Life throws curveballs, and some days feel heavier than others. But even on tough days, there's strength in choosing joy. It could be as simple as acknowledging your emotions, reaching out for support, or treating yourself with kindness. Remember, joy isn't a finite resource – it's abundant and accessible, waiting for you to embrace it. So go ahead, sprinkle joy into your day, and watch how it transforms your world.

Your Personal Growth Toolkit

So, you've made it to the section on personal growth – high five! This is where we lay down the tools and strategies for expanding your skills, mindset, and overall development. Think of this as your go-to toolkit for nurturing your potential and becoming the person you aspire to be. First off, let's talk about self-awareness. It's like the compass that helps you navigate the terrain of personal growth. Take some time for introspection, journaling, or simply reflecting on your experiences, strengths, and areas for improvement. Self-awareness fuels growth, so pay attention to your thoughts and behaviors. Next up, we've got goal setting. Setting clear, attainable goals gives you a roadmap to follow and something to strive for. Break them down into smaller milestones and celebrate each victory along the way. Then, there's continuous learning. Whether it's reading books, taking courses, or seeking mentorship, ongoing learning keeps your mind sharp and opens new doors of possibility. Don't underestimate the power of surrounding yourself with inspiring individuals. Cultivate relationships with people who uplift and challenge you, fostering an environment conducive to growth. Now, mental and physical well-being go hand in hand with personal growth. Prioritize self-care, exercise, and healthy habits to ensure you're operating at your best. Embracing change is another vital aspect of personal growth. Be open to new experiences, perspectives, and challenges; they all contribute to your evolution. Lastly, resilience – the ability to bounce back – is a key tool in your personal growth toolkit. Learn from setbacks, adapt, and keep moving forward. Remember, personal growth isn't a race; it's a lifelong journey. Each tool you implement contributes to your growth story, shaping you into the best version of yourself. Seize these tools with enthusiasm and make them part of your daily practice. Are you ready to unfold the next chapter in your personal evolution? Let's dive in!

The Next Chapter Awaits

You've reached the final section, and it's time to ponder what lies ahead. As you reflect on your personal growth journey, it becomes clear that life is an ongoing adventure with twists and turns waiting around every corner. The next chapter, like all great stories, offers both excitement and uncertainty, but it's brimming with opportunities for new experiences and fresh growth. Picture it as a blank canvas waiting for your colorful brushstrokes. One thing is certain: the next chapter will be filled with new lessons, new people, and new challenges. Embrace the unknown, for within it lie the seeds of greatness waiting to bloom. This is your chance to apply all you've learned, to stretch beyond your comfort zone, and to evolve into the person you aspire to become. Think of it as a surprise package waiting to be unwrapped. As you stand at this juncture, take a moment to acknowledge how far you've come. Celebrate your victories, big and small, for they have shaped you into the resilient, capable individual you are today. Remember, it's not just about reaching your destination; it's about relishing the entire journey, complete with detours and unexpected stops along the way. Think about the dreams and goals you've yet to chase and the ambitions that still flicker brightly in your heart. This next chapter presents the perfect opportunity to breathe life into those aspirations. It's your shot at exploring uncharted territories, embracing fresh passions, and fearlessly pursuing your deepest desires. There's a whole universe of possibilities out there – go claim them! Now, as you face the next chapter, carry with you the wisdom accumulated from your personal growth toolkit. Draw upon the resilience, courage, and insight that have guided you this far. Trust that you possess the strength to navigate whatever comes your way and harness the skills and knowledge you've gained, using them as tools to carve your path forward. Time to step boldly into the unknown, armed with the understanding that with each twist and turn, you'll craft a narrative uniquely yours, rich in experiences that weave into the fabric of your remarkable life story.

Did you love *The Anti-Hustle Building A Thriving Business On Purpose & Wellbeing*? Then you should read *Self-Coaching, Put On Your Life Mask Before Helping Others*[1] by Robert Jakobsen!

[2]

In "Self-Coaching: Put On Your Life Mask Before Helping Others," readers are invited on a transformative journey of self-discovery and empowerment. Drawing on the familiar airline safety instruction as a powerful metaphor for self-care and personal growth, this book explores the critical importance of addressing one's own needs before effectively assisting others. Through a series of insightful chapters, the author delves into the art and science of self-coaching, offering readers practical strategies for developing emotional intelligence, resilience, effective communication skills, and much more.

---

1. https://books2read.com/u/mZYrqJ

2. https://books2read.com/u/mZYrqJ

With a focus on building a solid foundation of self-awareness and self-compassion, "Self-Coaching" equips readers with the tools needed to navigate life's challenges with grace and to make positive changes that ripple out into their relationships, careers, and beyond. Whether you're a leader seeking to inspire others, a professional aiming to achieve new heights, or simply someone who wishes to live a more fulfilled life, this book serves as a guide to putting on your life mask first—ensuring you are at your best to support those around you.

"Self-Coaching: Put On Your Life Mask Before Helping Others" is not just a book; it's a roadmap to thriving in business and life, offering 17 habits every high-achiever must adopt to not just survive but truly thrive